Project Performance Review

Project Performance Review focuses on evaluating projects efficiently and in context, identifying important improvement opportunities and leading project and organizational management practices. It advises how these can be put in place to give stakeholders confidence in the control and delivery of their projects without waste.

The authors explain not just the mechanism and objective of project performance reviews but also the ideal environment in which they are intended to be implemented. The shaping of this environment, by the stakeholders and technical team, is key to achieving your intended outcomes. Without the professional cooperation of all interested and informed parties, the effectiveness of any review may be compromised. Topics addressed include: introducing the project review method, engaging project stakeholders, ensuring project governance, conducting project risk assessments, improving accountability, providing project assurance, organizing and managing projects, optimizing review scope and approach, avoiding review pitfalls, meeting existing audit standards, and proposing alternate approaches to project evaluation.

Dr. Alexia Nalewaik is Vice President – Major Projects and Program Management for WT Partnership. She has over 25 years of experience in risk assessment, owner representation, performance audit, and cost management. Alexia is Chair of the International Cost Engineering Council (ICEC) and is a Fellow of RICS Americas, AACE International, and ICEC. She is also a member of the American Society of Civil Engineers, IPMA-USA, and the National Association of Construction Auditors.

Dr. Anthony Mills is Professor of Construction Management and Head of School in the School of Architecture and Built Environment at Deakin University. He is a quantity surveyor and is currently National Vice President of the AIQS. Dr. Mills has published over 100 referred papers in international journals and conferences and is a member of several local and international Boards, including the Australian Council of Deans of the Built Environment. He is a founding member of the Australian Construction Industry Council's Construction Forecasting Council, and is a Fellow of the AIQS.

More than 50 years of research has shown that project cost and schedule outcomes are not improving. We fail to address what I call 'systemic risks'. Doing so requires that we capture learnings and apply them objectively to reduce risks and improve performance on projects and project systems as a whole. The book by Nalewaik and Mills provides a practical guide to a flexible performance review method that, if applied consistently, should take your project system from mediocrity to excellence.

John Hollmann, Owner, Validation Estimating LLC,
Author of *Risk Quantification* and Lead Author of the
AACE International *Total Cost Management Framework*.

Project Performance Review

Capturing the Value of Audit, Oversight, and Compliance for Project Success

**Alexia Nalewaik and
Anthony Mills**

Routledge
Taylor & Francis Group

LONDON AND NEW YORK

First published 2017
by Routledge
2 Park Square, Milton Park, Abingdon, Oxon OX14 4RN

and by Routledge
711 Third Avenue, New York, NY 10017

Routledge is an imprint of the Taylor & Francis Group, an informa business

© 2017 Alexia Nalewaik and Anthony Mills

British Library Cataloguing in Publication Data
A catalogue record for this book is available from the British Library

Library of Congress Cataloging-in-Publication Data
Names: Nalewaik, Alexia, author.
Title: Project performance review : capturing the value of audit,
    oversight and compliance for project success / Alexia Nalewaik
    and Anthony Mills.
Description: New York : Routledge, 2016. | Includes bibliographical
    references and index.
Identifiers: LCCN 2016016605 | ISBN 9781472461407 (hardback) |
    ISBN 9781315602424 (ebook)
Subjects: LCSH: Project management—Evaluation.
Classification: LCC HD69.P75 N35 2016 | DDC 658.4/04—dc23
LC record available at https://lccn.loc.gov/2016016605

ISBN: 978-1-4724-6140-7 (hbk)
ISBN: 978-1-315-60242-4 (ebk)

Typeset in Times New Roman
by Apex CoVantage, LLC

Contents

List of illustrations   vii
Preface   viii
Foreword   ix
Acknowledgments   xi
Acronyms and abbreviations   xii

1   Introduction   1
What is performance audit? 1
The need for project performance reviews 1
Types of projects that can be reviewed for performance 3
What makes this book different? 3

2   Discussion   7
The evolution of performance audits and reviews 7
How project performance review differs 9
Audits, reviews, and assessments 10
*Typical challenges experienced with project performance
    reviews 11*
Procuring the project performance review 26

3   The Nalewaik-Mills Performance Review Method   36
Refining the concept of project performance review 37
Economy, efficiency, and effectiveness 41
The project life cycle 42

4 Overview of the Nalewaik-Mills Performance Review Method   46

Module 1 – Planning 46
Module 2 – Stakeholders 51
Module 3 – Risk 56
Module 4 – Compliance 62
Module 5 – Resources 65
Module 6 – Management controls 67
Module 7 – Post-project 73
Module 8 – Special issues 76
Project performance review exclusions 76

5 Summary   82

The future of project performance review 82
Closing comments 83

Further reading   85
    Published works and presentations by the authors 85
    Other recommended reading 85
Index   87

Illustrations

Figures

3.1	Module relevance to project life cycle phases	43
4.1	Nalewaik-Mills Performance Review Method	47
4.2	Stakeholder mindmap	52
4.3	Types of risk	58
4.4	Risk management form	60

Table

3.1	List of project performance review modules	37

Preface

This book outlines a flexible framework for the scoping and implementation of project performance reviews, which often are required as part of oversight for projects. It is based on the principles of performance audit and is designed to comply with audit standards. It presents a process for improving performance reviews so as to both report on issues and begin a continuous improvement cycle for both current and future projects.

Concerns about fraud, waste, compliance, transparency, and organizational effectiveness have led to the use of performance review as both a governance mechanism and a continuous improvement tool. The goal of project performance review is threefold: (1) reduce project delivery risk; (2) improve transparency and accountability; and (3) increase organizational maturity. While performance audits, monitoring, and measurement have been conducted in government organizations and departments for decades, the specific application of performance review to projects and programs is fairly new.

In this book, the authors:

- Present their extensive experience and suggestions for undertaking performance reviews.
- Identify the gap between research and current practices addressed by the proposed model.
- Reflect on past audit scopes, challenges, and significant opportunities lost.
- Present a compelling framework for understanding the need for performance reviews as a vehicle to improve project outcomes and project organizations.
- Enumerate and genuinely embrace all significant positive aspects of performance reviews for the improvement of project management efficiency and effectiveness.

Foreword

There is a somewhat unkind interpretation that has become a form of humorous mythology of the role of those who undertake audits and reviews that can be expressed as follows: "An auditor is somebody who enters the battlefield when the fight is over and slaughters the wounded". Many organisations and agencies that undertake audits, reviews and assessments of projects have long since moved away from a focus on blind compliance, finger pointing and the search for the guilty and punishment of the innocent. The concept of audits as being focussed on only compliance is outdated and unhelpful. That quote still gets a few laughs, but thankfully we are all becoming more sophisticated about the role of governance, organisational learning and the importance on focussing on outcomes rather than being purely fixated on process and compliance. This book helps in broadening our horizons of audits, reviews and assessments to see the benefits that can be gained from such exercises.

Investigating what went wrong, or right, with a project provides substantial learning opportunities, which is a key benefit, but it is often poorly valued. This is unfortunate because understanding the mechanics of project delivery can provide valuable data for the detection of early warning signs on future projects as well as provide a wealth of valuable data to help trigger innovation and continuous improvement initiatives.

This book is invaluable for several reasons. First, it provides some constructive background context on the origins and evolution that is useful to understand; knowing the history of something is important. The terms related to audits and reviews are also introduced and explained in a very simple and effective manner. Second, the book provides an intelligent section on procuring audit services that discusses how these activities are undertaken and suggests how the practice may be improved. Third, it details a process of how to physically and mentally go about performance reviews in a mindful way which will take it beyond a compliance exercise to the level of knowledge harvesting and critical thinking so that continuous improvement can be the key outcome. It does not prescribe a step-by-step 'how-to' guide on undertaking performance reviews; instead it provides a scope guide to what should be included and how the philosophy of this kind of work may be shaped in a more sophisticated way, and it assists users of the book to understand what path they might take after the review to capitalise on the effort expended.

The book is targeted towards sophisticated practitioners with an interest in this area. It is well written, clear and jargon free so that practitioners who would like to become more sophisticated will find this a valuable resource. Similarly, for academic researchers, the book also provides a useful reference and framework. The authors are to be congratulated on finding a fine balance between oversimplifying the ideas presented while expanding the content of what is traditionally seen as a rather 'dry' subject, so that it can 'whet' the appetite to use the process more constructively and strategically.

Dr Derek Walker
Emeritus Professor of Project Management,
RMIT University, Melbourne Australia, 4th April 2016

Acknowledgments

We would like to express sincere appreciation to all the friends and colleagues who offered advice and assistance, especially Gerald G. Nalewaik, David Brady, and Christopher Rose for volunteering to critique in excruciating detail. Special thanks to Jonathan Norman for his unflagging faith and patience.

Acronyms and abbreviations

BREEAM   Building Research Establishment Environmental Assessment Methodology
COSO   the Committee of Sponsoring Organizations of the Treadway Commission
CPA   Certified Public Accountant
CSF   critical success factors
EA   enterprise architecture
EAC   estimate at completion
ECA   European Court of Auditors
EHS   environmental health and safety
ERM   Enterprise Risk Management™ COSO
ERP   enterprise resource planning
ETC   estimate to complete
EV   earned value
EVM   earned value management
FEED   front end engineering design
FF&E   furniture, fixtures, and equipment
GAGAS   Generally Accepted Government Auditing Standards, The Yellow Book
GAO   United States Government Accountability Office
INTOSAI International Organisation of Supreme Audit Institutions
ISO   International Organization for Standardization
ISSAI   International Standards of Supreme Audit Institutions
IT   information technology
KPI   key performance indicators
LEED   Leadership in Energy and Environmental Design
PMO   project management office
PRINCE2 PRojects IN Controlled Environments
QA/QC   quality assurance/quality control
RFP   request for proposal

RFQ   request for qualifications
ROI   return on investment
SME   subject matter expert
SOV   schedule of values
SOX   Sarbanes-Oxley Act
TCM   total cost management[1]
TQM   total quality management
VfM   value for money
WBS   work breakdown structure

Note

1 Technical Board. (2006). *Total Cost Management Framework*. Morgantown, WV: AACE International.

1 Introduction

The method presented in this book is framed as an approach to project review and is based on the principles of performance audit. It is also designed to comply with audit standards. The method is ultimately intended to be used to improve the project and project organization.

What is performance audit?

Audit and review are two of the oversight mechanisms most commonly used to provide assurance and give confidence to stakeholders. There are many types of audits: internal audit, expenditure audit, compliance audit, systems audit, financial audit, and more. No matter which type of audit is performed, it can be generally defined as a review of an organization's activities or accounts by either an internal department or independent external organization and a promise or guarantee (assurance) by the auditors that the accounts are true except as reported in the audit findings.

A performance audit, specifically, is intended to review the *Efficiency*, *Economy*, and *Effectiveness* of an organization in achieving a particular defined objective through the use of certain available resources and can be utilized as a vehicle for organizational improvement and maturity. Where traditional audits answer the question "Was it done right?" by verifying compliance with procedures, specifications, and systems and assuring or questioning the accuracy of accounting, the performance audit asks, "Was the right thing done?" and looks at the panorama of context, situation, intent of behavior, and actions undertaken in the course of achieving organizational goals. Performance audit and reviews complement other types of audit and are similar to operational reviews in that they consider not just the past and present but also the future.

The need for project performance reviews

Projects can experience dynamic change, which then results in overspending, delays in on-time delivery, reduced quality, and other such failings in achieving their intended objectives. Such failures can occur in any project type, sector, or industry. For most organizations, project funding is not unlimited, which creates a very real constraint on the project that is difficult to overcome when cost overruns occur. Projects are often created in response to a specific time-sensitive organizational need; where there is a hard deadline for the delivery of a product or opening of a building, this may be more important and critical to the organization than cost. If a project is performing well, reviews may be conducted at regular intervals as a preventative measure. However, any volatility or occurrence of an unrecognized significant risk creates an urgent need for immediate diligent oversight of projects, especially those that receive public funds or donations and thus require an even higher degree of transparency and accountability. An audit or review may be triggered in such circumstances.

Many types of projects and the teams that create them are unique, non-repeatable, diverse, and a bit unpredictable; these projects change constantly, often to the extent that change becomes the norm. Herein, a project is defined as a temporary organizational entity created to realize a specific goal; it is important to note that, whereas the project is temporary, the executing (Owner/client) organization or enterprise might not be. Traditional control mechanisms work most effectively when tasks are repetitive and predictable; some types of manufacturing projects lend themselves to this static control situation, in which change is planned and occurs during iterations. The trouble is, the world of projects is now so deep and broad that detailed rules, processes, and policies and procedures cannot be developed to cover all possible occurrences for all possible types of projects.

Very few if any projects are perfectly repeatable. Projects and systems that change rapidly do not lend themselves to a template. On dynamic projects, stakeholders must rely on the skills, experience, and judgment of the project team to make robust decisions, provide guidance and assurance, and call on experts as needed to provide timely investigation and advice.

Due to the magnitude of expenditure on major and mega-projects, termination often becomes unacceptable even when their extreme cost and schedule overrun become visible and/or the project viability is in question. It may be difficult for the project team or organization to admit defeat, accept the sunk costs, and exert the necessary authority to cancel the project, especially for very public or otherwise high-profile projects. There may be such a demonstrated or perceived need (especially where there is a public need) for the project that it cannot be cancelled at any cost. As a result, many projects continue to limp forward in the face of adversity, change, newly discovered risky conditions, slipped milestones, and ever-rising costs toward an unhappy conclusion. Project shocks and failures of the type mentioned may trigger the need for a performance review, wherein an independent team can consider the objectives of the project and attempt to recommend solutions to the issues raised.

Fortunately (or unfortunately) for most organizations, history, short memories, and positive spin tend in the long term to erase the label of failure, and measures of success are ultimately identified and promoted, even for projects that missed cost, schedule, and performance goals. The Sydney Opera House comes to mind as an example.

Increased stakeholder awareness of expenditures, conservatism, risk awareness, demands for transparency and accountability, and a greater focus on controls and obtaining value for money mean that stakeholders more often are turning to audits and reviews as a mechanism for control, risk management, and trustworthy reporting of project and organizational status. Stakeholders (especially the general public) have certain expectations of *Economy*, *Effectiveness*, and *Efficiency*, legality, ethics, stewardship, and equity; consultants performing the project review can report back to stakeholders on all of these and provide a judgment of whether the expectations are reasonable. Project review is an effective tool that can be used to support management practices and controls. The performance review method discussed herein provides a necessary assurance and pertinent advisory function to project Owners and their stakeholders alike.

Types of projects that can be reviewed for performance

Review mechanisms are typically designed to be generic, such that they can be applied to many different types of organizations and situations, and performance review is no exception. Although the authors' experience with performance audits and reviews is specifically in capital (construction) projects, the Nalewaik-Mills Performance Review Method presented here has been designed such that it can be applied to any type of defined and bounded public- or private-sector project, such as: government, information technology, construction, manufacturing, major events, and more. It can be used in any industry sector (e.g., education, healthcare, utilities, petrochemical, pharmaceutical, commercial, infrastructure) and in any country, county, state, city, or agency. It is flexible enough to be useful to projects, programs, and portfolios and the organizations that create them.

What makes this book different?

There is no shortage of project management literature available, each outlining various methods and best practices for managing projects and purporting to ensure successful projects. There are countless member-based professional organizations that provide support, guidance, forums, training, and certification to project managers and their ilk. Universities even offer academic degrees in project management. Project management is not a new profession, and yet projects continue to fail. Results seem to defy reason. A project that follows established policies and procedures precisely, monitors itself against metrics and benchmarks, and implements all the current best practices can flop. Similarly, a project that does little of this can, heroically, succeed. There are too many intertwined variables to claim that certain actions and activities will guarantee project success. The discipline of project management is evolving, but project assurance demands something more, and here performance review steps in.

Books written on performance management for project management professionals tend to focus on the use of key performance indicators and metrics. The majority of books and guidelines written on performance audit appear to be intended for persons in the accounting and audit professions, internal audit, or government or people who wish to be in those professions. Books on performance review do not specifically address the challenges of such reviews, specifically the performance of projects. Books on project audit tend to focus exclusively on expenditure and compliance auditing, even though compliance (with policies and procedures, laws, regulations, contracts, etc.) is not a guarantee of project success. While there are books on project and construction audit, some of those seem to be focused on teaching certified public accountants (CPAs) and auditors about key concepts in project management instead of actually describing how to audit projects. In the authors' experience, it is easier and more effective to teach project management professionals how to audit than it is to teach project management to an auditor.

Currently, there exists no universal, comprehensive methodology for performance audits and/or reviews. Guidelines are insufficient, journal publications are scant, practitioners are unregulated, and formal education is unavailable (one cannot receive an academic degree in performance auditing, and audit is not typically included in project management curricula). As such, methodologies continue to evolve, diverge, and (occasionally) regress; approaches taken by practitioners vary widely and unpredictably, perhaps at the expense of their clients.

There are a few exceptions in which published guidance on project performance audit exists in the form of manuals or written policies and procedures, usually developed by individual government agencies, counties, or cities and which can sometimes be found freely available on the internet. These have been designed specifically for use by those entities, reflect the specific nature, obligations, bureaucracy, and politics of those entities, and may contain guidance that is unique to the challenges and risks faced by those entities and their stakeholders. That said, some of these manuals do contain useful guidance that may be portable to peer entities and possibly even portable to other types of projects and enterprises. Of note is the 2015 European Court of Auditors (ECA) performance audit manual, which specifically differentiates among performance, financial, and compliance auditing, recognizes that the discipline of performance audit relies on evaluation methods, and emphasizes that performance audit requires auditor skills, experience, and education that differ substantially from those required for financial audit. This book is not intended to supplant such performance audit manuals, but it may be used to supplement them.

The Nalewaik-Mills Performance Review Method presented in this book[1] was developed in response to requests from both audit clients and practitioners for a flexible and relevant method specific to reviewing the performance of projects. It builds on several decades of audit and project management experience, a doctoral dissertation borne from seemingly never-ending frustration with lackluster audit findings and stakeholder expectation gaps. It draws from numerous works previously published by the authors on the topics of project performance, audit, assurance, governance, quantity surveying, project controls, project management, risk management, stakeholders, and quality assurance. The model is based on performance audit concepts and designed to comply with audit standards. It is designed to be flexible and modular, such that the review can be responsible and responsive to project and organizational needs at every milestone and beyond. The review can be used to supplement existing project management methods or stand alone.

This method isn't a collection of checklists, and this book does not teach people how to conduct a review via a step-by-step process. Rather, the modules presented herein can be used alone, combined, and applied on an as-needed basis in any order at any time. It is intended, specifically, to assist Owner entities and their consultants in developing the scope of the review, appropriately procuring project performance review services, and overcoming typical challenges encountered during project reviews.

The model presented here:

- utilizes strategic and organizational management concepts to fill the published guidance void
- incorporates key attributes of program evaluation, which bring together internal departments, internal and external stakeholders, best practices, and the achievement of long-term goals
- incorporates risk management and quality management techniques
- enables both systemic and substantive evaluation, resulting in both quantitative and qualitative findings

- simultaneously focuses attention horizontally across the life cycle and vertically through stakeholder and organizational levels on established goals and risks
- ties internal management processes and project oversight to desired outcomes, identifying opportunities for improvement, and linking decision making to strategic objectives

As such, it assumes a fairly mature enterprise and organization of project management, but it can also be used to bring an organization (especially start-ups and mergers) to a higher level of sophistication by identifying what is missing, recommending improvements, and streamlining processes to decrease variability, increase optimization, improve predictability, and reduce risk.

The book opens with a definition of performance audit in Chapter 1, and discusses the specific need for such audits and reviews of projects. It then engages the reader with a more in-depth discourse about how and why performance audit evolved over time and explains specifically why performance audit differs from financial and other types of audit and review. The authors describe in Chapter 2 some challenges they have experienced with past project performance audits and reviews and then offer advice on how best to scope and procure a project performance review in order to avoid some of those challenges. Chapter 4 presents the audit framework. Each module is then described at greater length and in context, with specific challenges identified, discussion of how those affect project performance, and a reveal of what other specific problems consultants might wish to look for during the review. The section closes with a discussion of what elements of review should be procured separately and not included in a performance review. The book then concludes with some thoughts on the ongoing evolution and future of performance review and a brief recap of what was covered.

Note

1 Nalewaik-Mills Performance Review Method, copyright by the authors, 2014.

2 Discussion

In the history of audit, performance audit and (specifically) the application of performance audits to projects are relatively new concepts which have evolved and developed in recent decades in tandem with the auditing and evaluation professions. This evolution was driven by shifts in social values and the growth of strategic management theory.

Chapter 2 describes how performance audits and reviews have evolved over time and then highlights some typical challenges and difficulties that are experienced when conducting performance reviews. The authors then offer advice on how best to scope and procure a project performance review in order to avoid some of those challenges.

The evolution of performance audits and reviews

A typical audit can be loosely defined as a review of an organization's activities or accounts. Most often, when the term 'audit' is used, it (almost by default) brings to mind a financial audit of accounting and expenditures. The same term might also conjure a mental specter of a big, scary auditor with colored pencils, green eyeshades, calculator, and coffee breath. The practice of audit can be traced back to the stock market crash of the late 1920s. Historically, public-sector audits were focused on financial accountability, internal controls, answerability, and fiscal regularity. By the 1950s, accounting and internal controls were considered to be satisfactory if an internal or external audit demonstrated past transactions were performed legally, formally authorized, and accurately and completely reported according to standardized accounting principles. Internal audit functions became the norm in public-sector organizations and private-sector companies alike. To this day, financial audit remains an important factor in the review of organizational accounting, certifying that financial statements fairly reflect the entity's financial situation and operations for the period reported and applying fixed standards and methodologies in the review of financial controls.

In the 1950s and 1960s, times of fiscal austerity led to public concerns about fraud, deception, waste, and integrity in government agencies, necessitating an evolution of audit and management strategy toward compliance, documentation, and internal controls for both detection and prevention of fraud. There grew the recognition that transactions, although formally authorized and performed legally, may be willfully and knowingly unnecessary or excessive. The 1960s saw an increase in efficiency auditing and, by the late 1970s, bureaucratic control was the public-sector norm. A desire for error prevention and fraud deterrence yielded internal controls developments such as codified policies and procedures for routine activities and segregation of duties, which could be readily audited for compliance. Regarding organizational performance, there was also a presumption that rigid adherence to prescriptive procedures would produce desired results; however, the art and science of performance and accountability prove to be far more complicated than a problem to be solved by merely following a roadmap or checklist.

In the world of projects, accountability is not the same as accounting, and public accountability differs considerably from financial accountability. Various other kinds of accountability exist on projects, including bureaucratic, legal, contractual, professional, and political accountability. Accountability often requires behaving within certain constraints, whereas performance sometimes requires innovation. Rules cannot be written to cover every possible situation; much in the world of projects is dynamic, and where there is a rule there is often a corresponding loophole. Audit methods used today are rooted in the 1980s and take a legalistic inspection approach to internal controls, including systems review and validation of compliance with both regulations and processes. These methods are most effective in repetitive, static, and foreseeable situations, whereas the world of projects can be considerably less predictable.

A trend toward conducting program evaluation and efficiency audits within government agencies reflected a desire for evidence of greater accountability for expenditures and successful delivery of services, answering the question, "Did we get what we paid for?" Expenditure audits and contract compliance audits became increasingly popular, testing expenditures and contractual activity for proper approvals and compliance with procedures, regulations, and contract terms. The desire for this type of audit endures, with a focus in the early 2000s on protecting shareholders and public interest. In the project world, project control began to be seen as analogous to financial and internal control for the specific project or program.

Accountability and performance are dynamic and sometimes conflicting concepts that require more than just a review of financial accuracy and compliance. The 1980s reflected the continuing evolution of audit and strategic management philosophy toward performance measurement, monitoring, and controls that focused on the achievement of organizational goals, practices that became codified in the 1990s. Unfortunately, it was soon shown that what was measured was most likely to be acted upon. Organizational and individual performance then became targeted toward achieving narrow objectives and specific measures of success instead of focusing on the bigger picture, with individuals, departments, and organizations alike motivated by the reward structure integral to established performance metrics. Strict performance measurement was even seen to be in conflict with the project quality objective. In the project world, these performance measurement mechanisms (metrics) still remain and proliferate. Metrics, critical success factors (CSF), and key performance indicators are discussed a bit later on in this book.

Also in the 1990s and into the 21st century, the substantive concepts of *Economy*, *Effectiveness* and *Efficiency* (the 'three Es' of performance audit) were introduced, enabling critical questioning of resource use and a boom in operations audits, performance audits, and evaluation research. The concept of *Economy* emphasizes an element of frugality and reasonability in the consumption of resources, *Efficiency* focuses on producing specific results while at the same time minimizing waste, and *Effectiveness* assesses the level of success in achieving the stated organizational goal. The definitions of the three Es have never been static or universal; while the keywords remain the same, interpretations can vary.

How project performance review differs

While for regulatory and statutory reasons audits of financial accuracy, controls, and organizational accountability persist, global movement continues toward the development of more sophisticated methods of performance assessment that blend qualitative and quantitative approaches, integrating both technical and social sciences skill sets. The project performance review method presented in this book is not a compliance-checklist method of auditing or agreed-upon procedures review, nor is it merely validation, although checklists can be (and often are) used to ensure comprehensiveness of examination. It has a wider time horizon than financial audit and internal audit and even attempts to look into the future.

Although audit can be a routine element in project oversight and monitoring, it is also often used as a tool for identifying the causes of (real or perceived) poor performance. It is an investigative mechanism that can be used for punitive purposes, although it has the potential to be used in many more beneficial ways during the life cycle of the project. The challenge caused by project failure is that the organizational and management response can be extreme. This is not necessarily the intent of project performance reviews.

Instead of concentrating purely on compliance, a project performance review tries to address the interdependent universe of resources (input), results (output), and impact. It focuses not only on inspection (compliance) but also on prevention of risk, quality, and performance issues. It takes a quality-oriented stance in review of the organization. By asking whether the right thing was done in a specific situation and focusing on context, this new focus on performance questions whether existing policies and procedures serve their intended purpose and determines whether controls and resources are appropriate, insufficient, redundant, or superfluous. It seeks sound administrative principles, remedied deficiencies, and positive impact of actions and decisions. It strives to make both the temporary project organization and the Owner organization ones of quality control, optimization, continuous improvement, maturity, and learning.

Project performance review considerably broadens the sphere of accountability beyond finance, controls, and compliance, to include the professional, personal, and political. It seeks to mitigate risk, satisfy stakeholders, and assure not just a better and more sophisticated project and organization but also a better future for the enterprise as a whole.

Audits, reviews, and assessments

The use of specific terminology, such as 'audit', 'review', 'assessment', and 'evaluation', varies from organization to organization. Some use the terms interchangeably; others are passionate about subtle distinctions between them.

Some clients may perceive an audit to be mandatory and a review to be voluntary. Others may view an audit as more rigorous and structured than a review, especially when it is conducted in compliance with audit standards. This is derived from the world of financial statements, wherein an audit is understood to provide a higher level of assurance than a review. Audits are generally perceived to be deep and reviews shallow. Note, this is perception, not necessarily reality; the authors have seen and conducted plenty of deep and comprehensive reviews, of the sort described in this book.

There is a similar distinction between the concepts of audit and assessment (or evaluation). 'Assessment' is a term often used in conjunction with concepts of quality and excellence. An audit is perceived to seek compliance with defined criteria and requirements, with a heavy focus on controls, whereas an assessment is seen to be more flexible, evaluating performance and appropriateness in a broader, nonprescriptive framework of concepts and principles. As with audits, evaluation standards and guiding principles exist and serve the purpose of ensuring the quality of management of the evaluation engagement. An assessment or evaluation may be perceived to occur periodically or on an ad hoc basis instead of prescribed or triggered. Performance evaluation is sometimes included under the broad category of performance audits.

While the Nalewaik-Mills Performance Review Method presented in this book is framed as an approach to project performance review, it is also designed to comply with audit standards. It is ultimately intended to be used to improve the project and project organization. Performance audit, by its very definition, considers elements of *Economy, Efficiency,* and *Effectiveness,* which makes it far more than just a validation of compliance; the project performance review method shown here, likewise, seeks to address the three Es and produce positive return-on-investment (ROI). As such, the intent of project performance review, as explained in this flexible methodology, also suits project performance audits, evaluations, and assessments.

Typical challenges experienced with project performance reviews

As with all things, there are elements that can affect the performance of the review team and the outcome of the review. A number of the elements discussed below were identified during a recent study that extracted factored data from more than 700 project performance audit and expenditure audit reports.[1] The effects of the factors were then objectively and empirically compared to the results of the audit in terms of type and number of findings. Others were identified through hands-on practical experience with auditing and observation of performance audit and review methodologies.

Certain issues are specific to the concept of project performance review, as differentiated from organizational performance review. The project and organizational environment in which project performance audits are conducted can be complex, complicated, political, dynamic, and situational. By definition, the term 'project' refers to the project (or program or portfolio) being reviewed, and 'engagement' refers specifically to the review. For the purposes of this book, a project is defined as a temporary effort (not ongoing operations), undertaken by a team or individual, which has been designed to achieve a particular goal. A project is typically comprised of a number of interrelated tasks that need to be performed within time, cost, and quality expectations. Here, quality is defined as a measure of how well requirements are met and thus how well the project is performing. A program is a collection of related projects, and a portfolio is the full group of projects and programs under the umbrella of the enterprise. When performance is improved on one project, those improvements may carry through to future projects, the program, and the portfolio and effect a culture change that spreads throughout the organization. As a result, there are both trickle-up and trickle-over effects on organizational performance as a whole.

Audit standards

There are various audit standards in effect around the world, adopted by government agencies and promulgated by professional institutions and lobbyists, which were developed primarily for the purpose of financial auditing. Some standards do exist for performance auditing; however, these tend to echo those written for financial auditing. Indeed, in the 2007 United States Government Accountability Office (GAO) *Generally Accepted Government Auditing Standards* (GAGAS, the Yellow Book), the standards for performance audits are included as chapters 7 and 8, part of a much broader document that also includes financial audit and attestation engagement standards. Similarly, the 2011 European Court of Auditors *Court Audit Policies and Standards* include performance audit as Section 2.2 of a document that also includes standards for financial and compliance auditing. In contrast, the International Organisation of Supreme Audit Institutions (INTOSAI) *International Standards of Supreme Audit Institutions* (ISSAI) 3000 exposure draft of September 2015 provides specific stand-alone standards and guidance for performance audit, separate from financial audit standards and other standards.

The majority of audit, consulting, and attestation standards create a framework for the planning and management of the audit engagement. Audit standards focus on such things as auditor ethics, independence, professional competence, quality control of the engagement, performance of field work, sufficiency of supporting documentation and evidence, workpaper quality, audit planning, and the reporting of audit findings. The use of such standards is intended to provide reasonable assurance regarding the caliber of engagement management, prevent litigation, and reduce audit risk (i.e., the risk of incorrect or incomplete audit findings, inappropriate or insufficient recommendations, and failure to detect fraud or other significant problems). Audit standards do not provide guidance on how to perform actual audit activities – for this purpose, audit manuals and audit guidelines are written.

The net effect of the adoption and heavy promotion of audit standards by professional institutions and governments alike is that laws, regulations, contracts, funding sources, and corporate policies frequently require auditors to apply accepted audit standards when conducting any audit engagement. In the United States, audits of projects that receive public funding are the only type of project audit that are statutorily required to follow GAGAS; yet requirements for the use of GAGAS continue to be part of the boiler-plate language used in the majority of audit solicitations, regardless of audit type, entity type, or funding source. Extant performance audit standards focus primarily on audits of governmental entities, not audits of nongovernmental entities or project organizations; as a result, performance audits that apply these standards tend to focus heavily on internal controls, information systems controls, fraud, and compliance. While use of these standards does not necessarily impact the audit in a negative way, requiring use of the standards may impact both the scope of work and the types of companies that submit proposals to perform the audit work. This and other issues with audit procurement are discussed later in the book.

The project performance review method presented in this book has been specifically designed to comply with the ISO (International Organization for Standardization) 19011 International Standard, Guidelines for Auditing Management Systems. Although there are no audit standards written specifically for project performance auditing and no standards for performance review, the typical project organization is comprised of governance mechanisms and systems for the purposes of project management. ISO takes a systems approach to management and a process approach to quality, with a focus on continuous improvement and a factual approach to decision making; thus the ISO 19011 standard is a good fit for this project performance framework. ISO standards are developed by consensus, with input from experts from all over the world, representing all disciplines, and are typically reviewed for update every five years. The ISO standard has the added benefit of being unrelated to (yet largely compatible with) more traditional financial and performance audit standards and being closely related to quality standards. In the context of the ISO standards, quality is a determinant of performance, aided by risk-based thinking. Key elements of the ISO guidelines include trust, auditor integrity, confidentiality, discretion, ethical conduct, fair presentation of findings, due professional care, independence, an evidence-based audit approach, continuous improvement of the audit methodology, thorough documentation and recordkeeping, and required follow-up and resolution of audit findings. Even though it is designed to comply with ISO 19011, the project performance review method presented in this book can also be used in conjunction with any other guidelines and standards, as needed by the client or as required by law; it is thoroughly compatible with performance audit standards such as GAGAS and ISSAI. Similarly, the review method presented here can be performed without applying audit standards, at the client's discretion.

Sampling and testing

It is necessary for reviewers and their clients alike to understand that the type of sampling can determine the quality, quantity, and type of findings discovered during testing. Sampling is the process of reviewing or observing a selection of something in order to better understand the whole population. It is often used in quality control/inspection (especially in manufacturing), statistics, and auditing.

There is often an element of expenditure testing in project performance reviews, wherein discrete expenditures are tested for compliance (usually contract compliance) and accuracy. However, testing can be inadequate, yielding some findings but not the deep insight that is required for a project performance review. This is due in part to the sampling method used, which is sometimes not conducive to understanding behavior on a project or project history. There are a number of sampling methods available during testing. In project reviews, sampling is often performed on a judgmental, random, or stratified dollar-unit statistical basis, but there are many other options available. Due to the nature of sampling methods, expenditure testing often selects and tests expenditures singly, out of context, and/or out of sequence. Lacking an understanding of expenditure history and evolution from period to period, the typical reviewer may not have enough information to properly question costs and change. They might not even be able to see trends on vendor and contractor invoices. Much more information is needed for the reviewer to appropriately and deeply evaluate expenditures on projects. Without more detailed information and context, the reviewer is only able to check math and cost coding, review line item expenditures against contract terms, find proof the expenditure is related to the project, and look for signature approvals, but not much more. Instead, the key elements of performance review (*Economy*, *Efficiency*, and *Effectiveness*) require that the reviewer be able to properly consider the context, appropriateness, and intent of expenditures and their role in the bigger picture of project success. Typical audit sampling methods do not always enable this.

The number of items sampled also impacts the review of the whole. For example, testing a high number of discrete expenditures differs from testing a high percentage of expenditures and yields a different kind of findings. While the reviewer can (and, when in a pinch, will) achieve review of a high percentage of total expenditures by selecting and testing only a few very large expenditures and then make some observations about controls and typical errors based on that random representative sample, this sampling does not necessarily give the reviewer deep insight into ongoing organizational behavior or evolution in behavior over time. Deep insight is what the performance review seeks, not shortcuts that reduce the consultant's required level of effort. The number of expenditures tested must be sufficient to offer an acceptable confidence level in achieving the review objectives. Testing a large number of discrete expenditures typically results in an increase in quantitative findings but also yields more qualitative findings and observations about organizational processes in the areas of procurement, finance, administration, and more.[2] We discuss, in the conclusion of this book, advancements in technology which may in the future allow reviewers to meaningfully test and model 100% of expenditures on a project.

Sampling can also be used to select other project documentation for review, such as contracts, change orders, timesheets, checklists . . . even projects, if a program or portfolio is being reviewed. In most cases, judgmental selection will be used for such documentation, guided by the client/ project team and risk, but random sampling may be appropriate in certain instances. Where project documentation is scarce, sampling may unfortunately be limited to what is available.

In short, the reviewer and client need to understand how the sampling method can impact the depth and breadth of review and choose the method that best suits the intent of the audit.

Size and duration of project

Project size and duration can be barriers to reviews, especially on very large programs with multiple projects, simply because data on small, short-duration projects is more accessible and less voluminous than the amount of information generated by major programs comprised of many projects that may span years. Mega-programs are difficult to examine; although there is no shortage of available data, the challenge is in targeting the right information to review, getting access to it, understanding the data and its context, and then figuring out what went wrong or right. Performance reviews do not always lend themselves to this type of deep and comprehensive testing and analysis, especially in organizations that resist the reviewer's presence.

The document request for a project performance review can be considerable and contains a myriad of items to be reviewed. On a small project with a duration of one year to 18 months, this may be relatively (comparatively) easy; a few purchase orders and contracts, a large handful of payment applications and invoices, some interviews, monthly project reports, some change orders . . . all this is readily manageable from an engagement management perspective. On a large program with multiple projects and multiple locations, this becomes exponentially more difficult, not just due to the number of projects but also due to the multiple levels of oversight required for the administration of such a large program. The reviewers will be required to obtain information from many sources, even if there is a project management office (PMO) or other centralized authority within the Owner organization/enterprise. Sometimes, certain program-wide information will be centralized at the PMO, while the remainder of information rests with the specific project teams. There may also be issues with obtaining data from the financial accounting system, as enterprise accounting systems sometimes capture information on only a fiscal year basis instead of a project life cycle basis.

Reviews of programs will necessarily differ from reviews of projects, and likewise reviews of portfolios. The reviewer may be faced with the likelihood of a shallow review of many projects instead of the deep review the program requires and questions that need to be asked about how the PMO or other oversight mechanisms impact the projects. A PMO is often created specifically for a group of short-term projects in which the Owner lacks the resources or where the types of projects are atypical for the Owner's core business. Not all project management offices are the same. The PMO is structured to suit the Owner's needs and may provide oversight and centralized administration for a group of projects, act as a buffer between the Owner and the project team, manage shared resources to projects, and/or behave as an Owner's representative, among other things. A PMO will add a new level of complexity to the enterprise and will create both bureaucracy and interdependencies. Depending on the nature of the PMO, the reviewer may choose to focus more on the PMO and project oversight than on individual projects, making the assumption that the PMO, policies and procedures, and governance have the biggest influence on team member behavior (and project performance). Indeed, approaches to and quality of project management and leadership at the project level might not even be seen by the reviewer, especially if the focus is on the PMO. The give and take of innovation and information between project-level, program-level, and site-specific teams might also be missed while the reviewer is busy focusing on the bigger picture. Insight to variability at the project level would provide considerable value to the organization. The review needs to be focused at an appropriate level of depth that matches the review intent; reading the PMO charter and objectives can assist in defining the scope and depth of review.

Due to the nature of consulting services procurement, reviewers are limited by the number of staff dedicated to the review and the time available for the review, including time and accessibility on site for gathering data and conducting interviews. The cost and time required to conduct an adequate project performance review will naturally be higher for certain larger projects and programs; if there are not enough funds allocated to the review, the breadth and depth of evaluation will be necessarily curtailed to suit the cost of performing the review. The authors have seen this occur time and again, especially where reviews are competitively procured and consulting firms provide their lowest-cost proposal in order to win the work.

As with sampling and testing, in order for the organization to obtain the maximum benefit from the performance review, the scope of the performance review needs to match the intent of the review and the approach needs to be tailored to the size and duration of the project or program in order to maximize ROI.

Reviewer independence

Reviewer independence is paramount. Performance reviews may be conducted internally (by employees within the organization) or by external consultants. In general, it is recommended that external consultants conduct the review to ensure impartiality, necessary skepticism, and objectivity. Independence has at its root two concepts: (1) disassociation from both the client organization and the project being reviewed and (2) an immunity to influence from the client or project team. In some situations, critical evaluation may be especially difficult, especially where the reviewer is reluctant to upset their prospects of future work from the client or the client is reactive to review findings and does not wish to disclose them (or shoots the messenger). Here, reviewer independence is vital.

At an individual level, the inherent biases of self-assessment are well known. Self-view tends to overrate actual achievement and performance, and thus individuals will typically score themselves higher on a self-assessment than would others. Simply put, people overrate themselves and believe themselves to be above average; the objective outsider does not suffer this problem of cognitive delusion when assessing an entity (although they probably suffer from the same overconfidence when assessing themselves).

This same phenomenon occurs in self-assessment of departments or projects; optimism runs amok within the project team and organization, especially early on, and (as with self-reporting of status on projects and self-evaluation) defects and failures tend to be downplayed. The self-assessment process can often be seen to be flawed, lacking in objectiveness. A self-assessment can result in an overly positive image of the project and over-confident prediction of performance, with few findings to act upon, a lack of meaningful feedback, and little contribution of value for the audit effort.

Such optimistic scoring isn't just self-protection; a desire to please (stakeholders and especially the general public), loyalty (to department, project, people, or company), and believing one's own press releases can also impact self-assessments. Even in an internal audit department, whose year-round mission purportedly involves unbiased inspection, politics may reign and impact both auditor independence and the contents of audit reports. The reviewer may encounter circumstances wherein the client requests two separate review reports: a detailed one for internal use and a redacted one for the general public or top stakeholders. Where the public report or presentation omits material issues and public funding is used for the project, this is clearly an ethics problem. The client organization may choose to deliver a presentation to stakeholders regarding review findings instead of the actual review report, effectively toning down and obscuring more severe language used by the reviewers. The client may even choose to combine findings from several review reports and investigations, further reducing and blurring stakeholder focus on the performance review. Delays in presenting the review report to stakeholders may also be an indication of internal sensitivity, pressure, or politics. All of these actions are an attempt at self-protection and appeasement of stakeholders.

The effects of self-aggrandizement and project team optimism are also directed at external auditors, a thin illusion that often fails to stand up to rigorous investigation. In interviews and questionnaires, skilled reviewers learn to expect and detect such behavior, overcoming it by questioning more deeply and requesting hard data and original data (not reports manufactured to best represent the project). They will also often encounter conflicting information and divergent opinions and will need to make sense of all of it, again with supporting documentation to establish the facts. This is where person-to-person interaction is an indispensable tool for the reviewer to gather information, look for issues that are mentioned repeatedly across a range of stakeholders, elicit information that is being carefully guarded, and review that information while at the same time trying to filter out bias, ulterior motives, and self-protection.

Although the authors have a clear preference for the use of independent external reviewers, a valid argument can be made that employees know the organization better than outside parties, are intimately familiar with the details and history of the project, and have the ability to report on circumstances that may elude an external reviewer, provided they are able to maintain an impartial stance and avoid internal politics even without complete independence. Some internal audit functions do conduct performance audits, with varying degrees of success. The client needs to decide what approach best suits the intent and mandate of the audit.

Availability of data

Whether the reviewer is an independent third party or internal agent, they will experience the challenge of obtaining and validating data. In order to be effective, the reviewer needs to obtain meaningful information received in a timely manner so they can intelligently evaluate the information and use it to develop actionable conclusions.

Client response to being reviewed can vary considerably, from a completely open-book approach that allows reviewers unfettered access to files and systems to a closed and guarded approach wherein the client requires formal requests for documentation and will provide nothing more than exactly what is requested and only if it is specified using the exact terminology used by the organization. Resistance to review may come from leadership, or it may be specific to the individual – this will make a big difference to the review, especially if the reviewer finds they cannot rely on leadership to motivate team members to comply with information requests. It may be useful for the reviewers to identify a sponsor at the outset of the review to whom issues and requests can be escalated. When leadership is invested in maximizing the ROI of the review, access to information will be improved.

Those being reviewed can make it especially difficult for the reviewer by providing only paper copies of documentation, even when electronic systems are used by the entity. To make it even more cumbersome, some clients have been known to provide PDFs of documents scanned with poor resolution, which then require the reviewer to recreate entire spreadsheets in order to validate data. Documents may be incomplete, out of order, hidden, lost, or missing in their entirety/shredded. People resistant to the audit might even take all the program files, jumble them, lock them in a filing cabinet, 'lose' the key, move the cabinet to a condemned building, remove all hard drives from the computers, and then announce that the auditors have unfettered access to everything. An alternate approach is for the project team to attempt to swamp the reviewer in volumes of extraneous information, often after delaying provision of the documents until it is nearly too late to complete the review, in the hope that the reviewer will get bogged down in the paperwork and be unable to perform the review effectively and within the time allowed. Reviewers need to be resourceful and tenacious in pursuing the receipt of project documentation.

Solutions to these problems include the development and use of a formal document request to both ask for information and track documents received by date and person. By sending the document request to all parties and copying their supervisors and/or the sponsor, those who are delinquent may be prompted (to avoid embarrassment or if ordered to do so by their superiors) into providing the requested information. Receipt of documents sometimes improves over time, as the reviewer gets to know the project team, gains their respect, and forms a bond. External data, such as press and project, community, or company websites, may be used as entry-level sources of information, such that the reviewer can utilize them as a springboard from which to request additional data. The reviewer may need to be creative and persistent, asking for specific information from more than one person in the hope that somebody will, eventually, provide it. If documentation is requested but not received by the end of the review, the reviewer can include this in their findings as missing information. When the reviewer then reviews the draft report with the sponsor, they may find that those documents appear for review post haste.

Metrics

Metrics are often used on projects and in reviews as a well-intentioned quantitative measure of performance. Metrics exist because we have a desire to simplify, codify, and quantify our world to make it easier to understand. However, they need to be very carefully defined and monitored lest they unintentionally provide a skewed perspective of the project. Just as metrics can drive good behavior, they can also result in bad behavior by providing unintentional incentives and an opportunity for strategic deception. Metrics can easily be misunderstood and misused.

Scorecard metrics, often used on program dashboard reports (addressed in Module 6 – Management Controls), provide a snapshot in time of progress and performance in the specific areas measured. These can be useful in determining the current status of certain elements of a project, compare information between projects on a program or portfolio, and can be used to develop a historical record. However, they might not effectively forecast performance or report on dynamics and risks, because they are often lagging measures subject to retrospective bias instead of leading measures.

To be measured, performance must be clearly defined. Critical success factors (CSF) are typically derived from project goals, which should be aligned with overall strategy and business requirements. Metrics and key performance indicators (KPI) must reflect these CSF. The purpose of metrics is to be used as tools for identifying and solving project performance problems and to guide decision making, not be an output in their own right. They should be predictive, quantifiable, actionable, and relevant.

Metrics that were meaningful on one project might not be appropriate for another project; they cannot be transferred easily and without contemplation from one situation to another. The relevance of metrics also changes throughout the life cycle of the project; different metrics are typically needed for each project phase.

If the project team has developed metrics for the project, the reviewers need to ensure they (the reviewers) do not accept the metrics blindly. Great care must be taken to understand metrics (what is included, what is excluded), how they were developed and what they were benchmarked against, the intent and methodology behind their development, and their relevance to and interdependence with individuals, departments, the project, the program, and the organization as a whole. This is because metrics are a proxy for the often abstract concept of success; they may exist because that is what can be measured, not what needed to be measured. Certain elements of organizational performance might not be observed directly, making them difficult to measure and even more difficult to measure consistently over time. Further, the metrics might not tie directly to the concepts of *Economy*, *Efficiency*, and *Effectiveness*, thus measuring something other than project performance. Metrics are not the only source of knowledge regarding relative performance, and the reviewer should not be overreliant on them when conducting the project performance review.

Metrics may also be overloaded, with one metric used for multiple purposes. This is an opportunity for the reviewer to determine whether more metrics need to be created. There is a delicate balance to be maintained when creating and using metrics; there need to be enough but not too many, and they should be kept simple. Further, metrics must be periodically reevaluated for fitness of purpose and appropriateness; metrics tend to become obsolete and provide less value over time. The performance reviewer can inquire about how often metrics are reviewed and updated to suit the needs of the project team as the project evolves.

Benchmarking

It is natural for an Owner to want to know how their project and organizational performance compare to that of their competitors or peers or even against themselves. Organizations seek to achieve successes similar to those of others; a benchmarked comparison assessment is an easy way for reviewers to compare project elements, milestones, management, and controls to others in the industry and document change and continuous improvement within an organization. Many reviewers include a benchmarking module as part of their review methodology. However, there are certain challenges and risks when conducting a benchmarking exercise.

Of the various types of benchmarking, performance benchmarking is the most generic, focusing on an output or goal and frequently relying on simple metrics such as cost, time, and output. As with metrics, discussed earlier, there may be no clear link between benchmarked data and the project performance qualities of *Economy*, *Efficiency*, and *Effectiveness*. Benchmarking begs questions of correlation and causation and a link to desired performance outcomes. When conducting a benchmarking exercise, the reviewer needs to ensure the benchmarking effort is relevant to the objectives of the performance review.

Competitors are easy to identify, true peers less so, especially in the world of projects. Certain Owners may clearly be considered peers in terms of industry or sector, but their projects and environment might not necessarily be similar enough to be truly comparable. Furthermore, due to competition within the industry or sector and the nature of proprietary processes and information, visibility of projects might not even exist, making benchmarking much more difficult and risky. Data may be difficult to find, and what is used for benchmarking may be whatever information is available instead of the best and most accurate information. If the reviewer does not know enough about the Owner's peer organizations, the benchmarking effort may be wasted by comparing projects against inappropriate others.

Performance benchmarking relies on reported data. Huge quantities of data are available from external sources, which is both a boon and a risk to consultants. Technology has made information readily available, but the quality of information may be suspect. Project reports, publicly available/ online data, and summaries of project information are often based on aggregate data from multiple sources within the project and organization and are particularly dangerous when used out of context and without thorough understanding of the information source, what is included and excluded, what information or background is hidden, and whether the data is intentionally misrepresented or optimistically reported. Data reliability and comparability are two of the biggest problems with benchmarking; the user assumes common definitions, terminology, and consistency in data collection, but those assumptions may be incorrect. Consultants need to understand how the data was developed and what is included in that data and recognize that it is wholly retrospective and possibly even very out of date. If performance benchmarking is being conducted as part of the review, it is imperative that the client specifically inquire of the consultant how the information was acquired, where it came from, whether they have personal/ professional contacts at those sources, and what depth of understanding they have regarding that data. The data must be reproducible and supported by documentation, not based solely on a verbal report or interview.

Process benchmarking, in contrast, is a broader and deeper effort that seeks to identify key operating practices for specific project types or work functions and may rely on lists of best practices. It requires greater effort and involvement on behalf of the reviewer to gather information that is often not publicly visible, perhaps through a document request or interviews. However, as addressed in Module 6 – Management Controls, processes are not merely plug-and-play systems; they must be adapted to the organization. Process benchmarking, when conducted with care, can provide considerable benefit to an Owner and project organization by resulting in recommendations for rapid procedural and structural changes.

Checklists of best practices

Because the concept of project performance cannot be defined without in-depth specific knowledge of the project and stakeholders, and because project reviews are naturally constrained by cost and time, many consultants will use checklists of best practices to ensure the project team is utilizing trusted project management methodologies (and also reduce their own required level of effort and time for the review). It seems a simple and quick way of ensuring necessary controls are in place, especially when reviewing governance elements as discussed in Module 6 – Management Controls. However, while checklists may be useful in jogging the consultant's memory about what to review, they can also lead the reviewer astray and render the review ineffective.

Although many successful organizations in highly competitive sectors and industries try to keep information closely held as a strategic differentiator and business advantage, the reality is that valuable processes and knowledge eventually trickle down and outward, diluting and adapting as they proliferate. Elements of organizational and management practice that once provided strategic advantage and garnered admiration are rapidly adopted by competitors, promoted within the profession, and spread by consultants and educational institutions as best practices. For this very reason, the authors sometimes refer to best practices as common or generally accepted practices, because the concepts have usually become so widely disseminated that everybody is using them.

One of the challenges with lists of best practices is this: Who developed the list of best practices and how? Who determined that these are best practices? A list may have been developed in house by the consulting or auditing firm, borrowed from a professional institution, found on the Internet, or may be an amalgam of all of the above, cobbled together from other sources. It may be more useful if it is specifically relevant to the industry, sector, organization, type of project, and life cycle milestone. Conversely, it may offer more value if it comes from a completely different industry or sector and you are the first in your industry to appropriate it.

Differences in adoption and implementation of such management practices can also have considerable impact on their *Effectiveness*, which means the use of management practices that were successful for one organization might not necessarily translate to a performance advantage for another organization. Further, due to project dynamics and complexities, there might not be a demonstrable, direct, straight-line relationship between best practices and project success. The *Effectiveness* of best practices tools is likely impossible to measure directly and independently; their impact on the project is not experimentally verifiable because there are too many other variables that are interrelated. Lack of proof that a best practice doesn't work isn't the same as proof that it does work. Borrowing good ideas . . . might not be a good idea, because what worked for them might not work for you. There might be correlation between best practices and good performance, but causality is difficult to prove. Does this mean best practices are useless for the purposes of project management? Not at all. It just means the project team and reviewers alike need to recognize that best practices function interdependently with many other elements to improve project performance, such as risk, project culture, and stakeholders. They are not the sole cause of project success.

Best practice review typically does not address their adaptation to the uniqueness or specifics of the project or program, and the resulting review tends to be shallow. The use of checklists during a review typically questions merely whether a management practice is in place or a specific type of document found without considering the quality dimension or usefulness of the best practice or even whether the processes are being followed. In order to be valuable as a performance review tool, best practices need to be evaluated not just for their mere existence but also for their quality of implementation, degree of institutionalization, and practicality. Furthermore, effective best practices aren't always free to implement, and the project team needs to demonstrate to the organization a return on that investment; application of superfluous best practices is a waste of time and money. If we think of best practices as resources for success and performance, we also need to think of and evaluate these investments in terms of their *Economy*, *Efficiency*, and *Effectiveness* on the project.

Forecasting mechanisms

One of the biggest challenges, in project reviews and project management alike, is the retrospective nature of review and reporting, which raises the question of how to forecast project performance. Data gathered for project status reports, regardless of report type, primarily includes data on what has happened on the project and try to present a picture of the current state of project progress. Consultants typically use these project status reports and other data to understand such items as the background of the project, issues, risks, stakeholders, and current conditions.

There are a number of project management tools that enable limited-range future forecasting on projects by extrapolating on current project performance. Some of these approaches are more sophisticated than others, but none are necessarily foolproof. It is certainly easier to look back on a project and discuss what happened than to try to foresee the future. Many elements of the investment decision-making process involve forecasting, as do elements of project management and project controls. Unfortunately, we seem to have a current shortage of oracles. History is different from knowledge, as it may well be skewed to reflect the preferred version of history, and historic information applied linearly might not be sufficient to predict the future. When strategic decisions are made based on planning fallacies or incomplete/inaccurate data (especially data based on unsubstantiated optimism or faith that the project will recover despite past performance), both the project and the organization suffer the unintended consequences. The consultant needs to understand how forecasting has been used for strategic decision making and can use this information as part of their review in Module 1 – Planning.

The primary mechanism for project forecasting is risk management. As discussed in Module 3 – Risk, this includes identifying project risks and their potential effects on the project. When risk management is taken to a greater depth, risk identification and analysis are used to develop a risk hierarchy, in which risk probabilities and impacts are quantified. Risk may also be modeled in a Monte Carlo type of mathematical simulation, with outputs used to help develop amounts to be applied to the project in the form of cost and schedule contingencies. These will be used to offset risk, based on the likelihood of risk occurrence and assumed potential values for cost and schedule elements. As with most things, the quality of the model depends on the quality of the data input, which in turn relies on both expert opinion and accurate project information.

On some project cost reports, the project team may include a data point called an estimate at completion (EAC) or estimate to complete (ETC). As with the Monte Carlo model described in Module 3 – Risk, the EAC relies on a quantification of the current understanding of project risk. The EAC is a cost forecast for the project, which will change over time and approach the actual project cost as contracts are committed, risk reduces, and the project nears completion. The EAC may be calculated using a formula that considers actual costs, projected budget, and performance information (an earned value technique discussed in what follows). It may even be based solely on an individual's opinion. In the latter case, the outcome is heavily dependent upon the skill and breadth of experience of the person, who might not be an expert. The EAC may shape behavior on projects in a reactive sense. The consultant can use these project cost reports not as a forecasting tool but as a way to understand how they impact project team actions and decision making.

Project reports are most often used to identify areas of change on a project, whether those be cost, schedule, quality, safety, quantities, or anything else that is measurable. Plotting this information over time (such as the EAC) can yield a trend line that can be used as a rough forecast of future performance. Use of such a trend line assumes the project conditions that caused the change will continue to impact the project in the way they have previously, undeterred. As change is often a constant on projects, every action has a reaction, and many variables impact performance, trend lines can be useful in the short term but become increasingly less reliable for projections in the longer term. Many of these techniques are based on the assumption that existing patterns of performance and behavior will continue. Turning points, wherein the project experiences a change in performance or behavior, can be difficult if not impossible to forecast. Unfortunately, project forecasting and trending are imperfect arts that rely heavily on the accuracy of project data, excellence in risk analysis, and the human judgment to predict future turning points. The reviewer should not assume that models and trend lines are an accurate predictor of future performance and should evaluate whether use of the mechanism adds value and whether reliance on such tools is appropriate or excessive.

Variance analysis plots what has happened on a project against what was expected to occur. A slightly more sophisticated method of variance analysis is earned value management (EV or EVM) and reporting. This is a progress monitoring and performance measurement tool that utilizes schedule, budget, actuals, and percentage completion information to compare actual and planned performance and project an outcome. Monte Carlo simulation may also be applied to EV as a forecasting method. However, while these methodologies report on physical progress measurement and variance from plan, they do not necessarily provide information about why performance is different than what was planned; as with metrics and benchmarking, these are tools for project management, not ends in themselves.

Such tools may be useful to the reviewer by shining a spotlight on areas in which there is actual or forecasted variance that should be reviewed in greater depth. The reviewers need to understand how forecasting methods are used by the project team. As part of Module 1 – Planning, Module 3 – Risk, and Module 6 – Management Controls, auditors should investigate the characteristics of trending and forecasting mechanisms to identify areas of risk inherent in the methodologies and degree of reliance on such tools when managing the project.

Procuring the project performance review

In order to best define the scope of the review, phrase a solicitation for services, and select the review team, the client organization needs to understand the factors that can potentially impact review results. The majority of review engagements are necessarily subject to constraints of cost and time, which can restrict the scope of the review, limit the amount of testing done, or prompt the client to select the lowest-cost proposal. In this book, improvements in the selection of a consultant team and the scoping of performance reviews are seen as integral parts of the solution to improving engagement quality, increasing the number of material (meaningful) findings, and positively effecting organizational maturity by prompting corrective and preventative actions.

Agency theory

The challenges inherent in the principal–agent relationship are particularly important in the procurement of consultancy services. In this setting, an agent (the consultant) is contracted to and acts on behalf of a principal (the client), who may themselves be agents (management) acting on behalf of a company or a very large body of principals (such as public stakeholders/taxpayers). The relationship between consultant and client is subject to the classic agency problem of information imbalance, described in what follows.

In winning the work, the consultant has given the client a sales pitch, which may or may not reflect the reality of their ability, possibly even promising the client the findings will allow them to recover expenditures and thus offset the cost of the review in whole or in part. The authors are personally familiar with some firms promising returns of up to 20:1. In the authors' experience and the aforementioned study of 775 audits,[3] the amount recovered from a performance audit is, typically, zero. If a large amount is questioned, it is likely either a single big error was found or an error became material because it was repeated each month and propagated throughout the duration of the project. Clients should not believe the sales pitch that monies recovered from review findings will completely offset the cost of the review. It does happen, but rarely; it is the unicorn of reviews.

The principal–agent problem begs the question of whether the principal's interests can be ever really adequately served by the agents with whom they have contracted. Of course, the consultants know far more about themselves and their true abilities than the client. They may even know which audit or consulting firm would have been a better choice for the job, although they certainly would never tell the client. They know whether they will choose, upon winning the engagement, to substitute junior staff for the more expensive experienced staff whose resumes were included in the written proposal (known as 'bait and switch'), fail to use the third-party consultants who were proposed as part of the team, and judgmentally select a few high-dollar expenditures to review so they can show they have examined a high percentage of expenditures without admitting they actually avoided looking at the large pile of invoices that was available. Consultants can be skilled mercenaries, and clients are their prey. They know whether they will be taking a loss on the engagement that they priced extremely low to win the work, with the intent to later increase the review scope or claim extra cost of the work, use this opportunity as a toehold to create an enduring relationship with the client that will make profit over the long term, or leverage a high-profile client on their resume and in press releases in order to get even more clients.

The review mechanism is one of feedback, and thus the principal–agent problem is especially important if the review is compromised by lack of independence, inadequate scope, and/or inadequate expertise. In such a situation, the review can potentially endanger the client by obscuring threats and failing to identify opportunities for organizational improvement. Some agency problems may be mitigated by training, licensing, certification, mandatory continuing education, and ethics codes that purportedly raise the bar for performance and competence; many of these are the core of member-driven professional institutions.

The true quality of the agents, such as productivity, diligence, pertinent experience, and integrity, are usually obscured from the principal. Careful procurement of review services tries to overcome this by requesting information useful in differentiating consulting firms, conducting in-person interviews of potential review teams, identifying the skill sets of specific review team members by obtaining resumes, checking references, avoiding fee structures that are contingent on the review to recover monies, and including contract terms for the engagement that prohibit a bait and switch of proposed team members and guarantee individual reviewer availability. By developing an understanding of the specific expert services required, carefully defining scope, selecting only standards and procedures that are applicable to the situation, and applying criteria that limit the amount of discretionary behavior available to the agent, the principal can partially overcome the problem of inappropriate review proposals and improve the performance review engagement.

There is, of course, another problem with hiring consultants, which is true for consultants of every type. The procurers may not know what the consultants are really doing once they are selected, even if the client has required periodic status reports from the reviewer. There is an assumption that, because the reviewers' reputation is closely tied to the quality of their work, they will to some extent self-regulate their conduct and thus will behave ethically and self-monitor the quality of their field work and work product. Audit is fallible and offers only reasonable assurance. When audit errors are discovered, the auditors often deflect responsibility by adding qualifications, caveats, and notes.

The client can partially overcome some of these problems by cautiously crafting and managing the procurement process for the review engagement. The scope and language of the request for proposal should be very carefully written as discussed in what follows. Consultant proposals should include staff resumes and a guarantee there will be no bait and switch of proposed staff. Letters of recommendation are a first step but are not sufficient for the vetting process. Client references should be contacted directly and a questionnaire developed to more deeply probe their experience and satisfaction with the consultant. Likewise, a series of questions should be developed and finalist proposers required to appear in person for an interview. Key proposed staff should be included in the interview process. Too often, only senior management and sales staff represent consulting firms at such interviews, and the client loses the opportunity to get to know the people who would really be doing the work. During the engagement, the client should require periodic reports from the consultant regarding progress made, issues they have identified, and any difficulties they have had in conducting the work.

Scope

It can be argued that the single most significant element impacting review results is the review scope itself. Review scope is often driven by some organizational objective, whether it is to satisfy an audit or review mandate, investigate specific circumstances or concerns, or act as a catalyst for change. As such, review scope will naturally vary to suit the situation. It may involve a review of expenditures, metrics, a contract or portion of a contract (such as change orders), project, program, portfolio, department, deliverable, or any combination thereof. Generally, it can be said that broadly scoped reviews yield more findings, many of which will be qualitative; this tends to occur when there is more to a review than only a review of compliance.

Determining what to include in the review scope has a consequence; that is, determining what to include in review scope naturally also determines what not to include in review scope and can limit the consultant's ability to investigate. Of the many types of reviews, agreed-upon procedures engagements have the most restricted scope. In contrast, performance reviews can have the most expansive scope.

Key to scoping the review is an understanding of the intent of the review, level of organizational commitment to review, intended audience for the review, and stakeholder expectations of the review. It is not uncommon, when an audit report is produced, for an 'audit expectations gap' to be discovered, wherein stakeholders comment that the audit scope did not cover what they expected or the audit as conducted did not include the depth and breadth of review promised. This can be especially true with performance reviews; the authors have seen many instances in which a review of *Economy*, *Efficiency*, and *Effectiveness* was promised but only a bird's-eye review of compliance and/or best practices was delivered. Performance reviews that produce reports containing zero findings are a particular cause for concern from a performance improvement perspective. The review scope needs to be carefully matched with the client's and/or stakeholders' needs and the review objectives clearly stated.

A performance audit or review may be required by law, requested by governing boards or oversight committees, related to a suspected problem, or required by corporate policy because the practice has been institutionalized as a good practice. Events internal or external to the project may also trigger a performance audit or review, such as product failure, information security leaks, customer complaints, accidents that resulted in injury or death, fraud or theft, or an environmental incident related to hazardous material release. When scoping the review, the trigger or impetus for conducting the review should be clearly stated, and the review scope and methodology need to be carefully matched with the review mandate.

That said, review scope also impacts review cost and time, and engagement ROI tends to drive review scope and methodology, which then results in the lowest common denominator of review scope, consultant time, review team experience, and investment of effort. Indeed, it is far easier and cheaper to conduct a systems-focused and checklist-based compliance audit than to do a broad and deep review of project performance. Review scope is often reduced because of failure to understand the potential return on investment, which in project performance review will be both qualitative and quantitative. It is easy to understand the value of questioned expenditures and more difficult to put a hard-dollar value on improved processes.

Developing an appropriate scope for the review requires careful thought about the purpose of the review and a discussion about the cost benefit of including additional areas of review. Desired areas of review may need to be prioritized and scoped/addressed in separate reviews instead of all at once. Targeting review scope to stakeholder concerns and known risks is a good rule of thumb, as is discussed in Module 1 – Stakeholders and Module 2 – Risk in order to avoid a too-broad or too-shallow review scope. In this method, some review elements may fit in more than one module, which allows some flexibility when scoping the review and choosing which modules to include, and also gives the consultant some flexibility when preparing the report.

Once the review objectives are stated and the review scope determined, the reviewers can work with the client to develop review questions that suit the purpose of the review. They can then direct review efforts and resources to matters of significance. The consultants will also tailor their review methodology to the review triggers and focus, using results-, problem-, and systems-oriented approaches in combination as most appropriate and effective.

Timing and duration

Similarly, the timing and duration of the review, as it relates to the project and fiscal year, will have an effect on review results. Keep in mind, depending on the magnitude of the project, a detailed performance review may require several months of interviews, document requests and review, investigation of the status (resolution) of past review findings, and report writing.

Due to the duration of the review, findings regarding expenditures and procedures may become outdated before the review report is produced, especially if the project team is aware of the review findings and is motivated to begin remedying issues as soon as they are identified. Although this is a good thing in terms of organizational maturity and improved processes, it can be frustrating for the review team (especially when it results in fewer findings, which can then reflect on the review team as a job not well done). A good solution to this problem is to reflect such findings in the review report as having been earlier identified and quickly/satisfactorily resolved, giving credit to the project team for their prompt response.

Some performance reviews may be conducted on a fiscal year basis. However, documentation from year-end closing is not typically available immediately; it can take a couple of months for some reports and data (especially analytics) to be reconciled and produced. In fact, some ERP systems do not have the ability to track project expenditures on a project life cycle basis, requiring considerable workarounds at fiscal year-end, which will naturally delay receipt of information for the review. If generation of information for the review causes a delay in performing the review, additional project data and information will typically have been generated after the year-end close. If the consultants identify findings related to these post–year-end documents, the client will need to make a decision about whether to hold those findings for the next year's review (by which time the issues may have been resolved or the situation may have gotten even worse), reflecting in the current review only the time period through year-end. Including in the report current activities through the time of report finalization, regardless of date, results in a truer representation of program oversight at the time of report issuance. This issue is especially sensitive to qualitative findings about policies and procedures and best practices, where processes have improved since fiscal year-end close and show organizational evolution from lessons learned. This is an instance in which review timing is at the expense of the review findings, because restricting data to only that of the fiscal year effectively delays observation, praise for good practices, and resolution of issues. A solution to this challenge may be use of a preliminary report to provide an intermediate mechanism for reporting improvement and potential improvement opportunities.

Where timing and duration can potentially impact the review, the client needs to make a determination with the reviewer about how best to approach the data set and reporting of issues. Keep in mind that the entity may be required by a regulatory mechanism to report on only activities and expenditures during a particular fiscal year.

Review team composition

The type of auditors and specialist consultants included on the performance review team has significant impact on the quantity, quality, and type of review findings. The client needs to remember this when reviewing proposals from consultant teams and carefully consider the review objectives and mandate to select the most appropriate reviewers when soliciting proposals.

Many organizations, by default, include in their solicitation a boilerplate requirement that an audit or review be conducted by an accounting firm or (at the very least) include a certified public accountant (CPA) on the team. The language may even state that the team must be led by a CPA and the report and findings must be reviewed and accepted by a CPA managing partner. This is a carryover from financial audit and might not be appropriate for a performance review. Indeed, if such language is used in the review solicitation, it will have a considerable impact on the type of companies that propose on the work and may even discourage some firms from proposing, as discussed in what follows.

An auditor-accountant is expected to be knowledgeable about business management in general in addition to having deep knowledge of accounting and auditing but is not generally expected to have significant expertise in any other profession or occupation. Skills in accounting and financial auditing have their place on a project performance review team, but the particular auditor-accountant skill set does not readily lend itself to performance review or substantive evaluation of projects. It has been shown that, where accountants comprise the bulk of the review team, the majority of findings are routine controls and accounting issues.[4] This is because auditors with an accounting background tend to focus on what they know – procedural failures, compliance violations, missing documentation, mathematical mistakes, and coding errors. These are important from an organizational standpoint, and the quantified findings may well be material such that they impact project and financial reporting, but these are not necessarily the key to project performance. The knowledge base required for performance review is quite different, even more so for project performance review, in terms of both specialized knowledge of the project type and the nonfinancial/accounting investigative techniques required to conduct the review.

Specialized, functional industry- and discipline-specific knowledge should be a requirement for members of the review team for any project performance review. To clarify: individuals with actual work experience (and possibly even experience- and exam-based specialty certifications) in the project industry, not accountant-auditors who have simply performed audits in that space and claim to know the sector and industry. Consultants with specialized expertise in the sector, industry, discipline, and project type should be project-related subject matter experts (SME). They should have in-depth knowledge of and hands-on experience with the type of challenges faced by the project organization and thus may be better able to identify project risks, best practices, and stakeholder concerns. They should have direct access to industry and sector peers for external benchmarks (and information about what is included in that data), and not just benchmark by relentlessly surfing the Internet. They should be able to reach into their hat and pull out not a rabbit but lessons learned from previous reviews in that industry and sector of true or near peers of their client.

Knowledgeable specialists will be better able to earn project team trust by establishing credibility, primarily through one-on-one interaction and interviews, especially where those being reviewed have a deeply ingrained distrust of auditors. Gaining the trust and respect of the project and organization team will enable these knowledgeable specialists to elicit more valuable evidence of project challenges, encourage people to volunteer information, decrease resistance to the review, and enable meaningful and deep discussions. These individuals with specialized and functional industry and sector knowledge might not be full-time auditors; they may be consultants who lend their skills to reviews on an as-needed basis. Studies have shown that there are significantly more quantitative findings and also more qualitative findings where industry professionals are included as part of the review team.[5]

The ideal review team should include individuals that represent a combination of skill sets and depth of experience, including appropriate subject matter experts, accountants and auditors, data analysts, social scientists, and people with evaluation techniques such as interviewing and forensic investigation. Of course, there will be a tradeoff in review cost, as specialists can be expensive. The client will need to consider the return on investment, both qualitative and quantitative, when selecting the review team.

Language used in the solicitation

Very few departments or individuals wish to reinvent the wheel, and as such many organizations tend to ask their accounting or internal audit departments to write the solicitation for project audit and project review services. This is likely because those departments have already written and conducted other solicitations for audit services, and the organization naturally assumes the language used will be similar. Unfortunately, these departments tend to use the language and scope with which they are most familiar, which is that of financial and internal audit, regardless of their appropriateness. Terms such as 'single audit', 'yellow book', and 'agreed-upon procedures' are typical for financial and compliance audit but are inappropriate for performance review, yet they appear in performance review solicitations with alarming frequency. The review solicitation may include boilerplate requirements that impact the type of companies that propose on the work, such as financial, compliance, and internal audit terminology.

Organizations need to understand that the language used for soliciting review services will impact the team composition, type, and caliber of firms proposing to conduct the review. Requesting that an accountant be on the review team, as mentioned earlier, may result in proposals from more accounting firms than other consulting firms. Inviting a single audit, agreed-upon-procedures audit, or yellow book audit will likely result in responses from audit practices and may inadvertently exclude project consulting firms. Requiring compliance with certain audit standards may have a similar effect, as discussed. Other language may draw proposals from large companies instead of small companies, global businesses instead of local businesses, claims and consulting practices instead of audit partnerships. If it is the organization's intent to attract a certain type of firm, such as a claims or management consulting firm instead of an accounting firm, they should include in the request for proposal (RFP) or request for qualifications (RFQ) any keywords that are typical for that type of firm. Interview questions can be crafted to more deeply probe the proposer's philosophy, approach, unique skill sets, and depth of experience. Evaluation criteria, used to score and rank the proposals received, can be designed and weighted to attract proposals from the best-qualified firms. As a rule of thumb, the more generic the solicitation, interview questions, and evaluation criteria, the more broad the resultant field of proposers.

The formal solicitation must be very carefully reviewed for appropriateness to ensure what is requested is really what is intended and needed. When writing the solicitation, it may help for the writers to read what they have written as if they themselves are the proposer and consider how what they have written might affect their desire to propose or how they would craft their proposal and team. The language used must explicitly match the review objectives and satisfy the audit or review mandate without including detrimental boilerplate language, including the aforementioned standards, scope, timing, duration, team composition, and more. However, the language also needs to be specific enough to protect the client's contracting and procurement process – no doubt, some of the boilerplate language in companies' written solicitations has been crafted or at least vetted by their legal department. It's probably best to not delete that. The language needs to be broad enough to appeal to different types of companies, not just accounting and audit firms. Too often, we have seen audit expectation gaps that were unintentionally caused by the solicitation itself through a failure to communicate intent and expectations or even a conflict between boilerplate requirements and review scope, which resulted in incomplete proposals, inaccurate fees, the wrong team, and ultimately an insufficient review.

Notes

1 Nalewaik, A. (2013). Factors Affecting Capital Program Performance Audit Findings. *International Journal of Managing Projects in Business*, 6(3), 615–623.
2 Nalewaik, A. (2013). Factors Affecting Capital Program Performance Audit Findings. *International Journal of Managing Projects in Business*, 6(3), 615–623.
3 Nalewaik, A. (2013). Factors Affecting Capital Program Performance Audit Findings. *International Journal of Managing Projects in Business*, 6(3), 615–623.
4 Nalewaik, A. (2013). Factors Affecting Capital Program Performance Audit Findings. *International Journal of Managing Projects in Business*, 6(3), 615–623.
5 Nalewaik, A. (2013). Factors Affecting Capital Program Performance Audit Findings. *International Journal of Managing Projects in Business*, 6(3), 615–623.

3 The Nalewaik-Mills Performance Review Method

Given the need for performance review demonstrated earlier, and the known challenges with existing review approaches, scoping, and procurement, the question becomes one of how the performance review mechanism can be improved, with the ultimate goals of identifying opportunities for continuous improvement, goal-achievement assurance, and stakeholder satisfaction regarding sufficient oversight, accurate status reporting, expenditure controls, and risk management.

The flexible and modular approach presented herein advocates an assurance-based approach to performance review scope and procurement that focuses specifically on project governance, accountability to stakeholders, and risk mitigation as key elements of project success. The model is grounded in experience, supplemented by both historic and empiric research, and has been successfully realized in practical application. This method is specifically designed to adapt to any industry, sector, and geography and any size project, program, or portfolio. It is intended to satisfy regulatory requirements for audit, meet stakeholder expectations of review rigor and depth, and enable customized investigation while considering risk, risk tolerance, definitions of success, delivery of value, and the three Es of *Economy*, *Efficiency*, and *Effectiveness*.

The approach does not utilize a highly prescriptive template or checklist; it is responsive to the dynamics and uniqueness of both the project and the organization. The performance review scope and approach need to be malleable – able to be configured to suit the specifics of the organization being reviewed. By utilizing a flexible and modular approach, the review scope can be fine-tuned to address the explicit needs of the project and organization and review resources directed to areas that can benefit the most from the investment in review.

The methodology includes eight audit modules, each of which is described in its own section in chapter 4 of this book. Each of the modules can be selected as appropriate for the specific phase of the project life cycle and the needs of the project and organization. The performance review does not necessarily

Table 3.1 List of project performance review modules

Project performance review modules	**1. Planning** Matching objectives with long-term strategy
	2. Stakeholders Defining success
	3. Risk Optimizing opportunities
	4. Compliance Responding to internal and external requirements
	5. Resources Focusing on economy and efficiency
	6. Management Controls Improving effectiveness
	7. Post-Project Customer satisfaction and future planning
	8. Special Issues Targeted review of specific concerns and risks

need to include review of all eight modules at one time. Rather, the intent is for only the most necessary modules to be selected as needed at the initiation of the review. When reviews are conducted in subsequent review cycles, depending on the findings from previous reviews, new modules may be added, some modules could be skipped, certain modules might be revisited, and the status of previous review findings reviewed.

These modules should not impact the typical review process in any way. It is expected that the review still will include such activities as a kick-off meeting, document requests, interviews and/or workshops, review of documentation, development of findings, meetings with the client to discuss findings and issues, and a formal report and presentation. Consultants will still be expected to have access to systems, documents, and the ability to observe the projects and project team in situ. The method presumes all pertinent solid evidence and documentation are available to the reviewers (if they aren't, that will be an review finding), who will then use those in conjunction with observation and interaction with the project team to develop persuasive and actionable recommendations.

Refining the concept of project performance review

Why refine the concept of performance review? Because a static review model is ineffective in the project world, where projects have life cycles and change happens. Because many project reviews occur on an annual or fiscal year schedule with zero relationship to the project life cycle. The majority of project reviews are conducted at project closeout, surfacing findings too late to have any meaningful impact on the actual project, which makes the project review more about the organization going forward than about project performance.

As mentioned earlier, reviews tend to look backward instead of forward, an ex-post process that evaluates and reports on what has happened. Often, performance data is gathered at a single point in time, which creates a snapshot of the project at just one moment, out of context, telling us nothing of the evolution of the project or history apart from the pure variation from cost and schedule baselines. Project reports will reflect progress per year or period to date, but sampled documents will reflect human behavior at a point in time. From a practical standpoint, this is how reviews are conducted. However, project performance and human behavior are not discrete events; performance is a continuous process, with a cycle of ebb and flow. A new methodology contained herein is needed, one that can be responsive to the nature of the project, which looks at trends and takes more of an ex-ante approach to project performance while considering causality and the ever-changing nature of risk. Review findings may even be captured as part of the project's 'lessons learned' report.

The intent of this new approach to performance review is threefold: (1) to facilitate learning within the project and client organization, (2) to remedy issues that are discovered in the review at points in time during the project life cycle when processes can still be improved, and (3) to result in better project, team, and organizational performance. The Nalewaik-Mills Performance Review Method achieves this by significantly broadening the definition of what can be assessed beyond just the typical cost and schedule metrics. Any consumption of project resources (staff, equipment, software, materials, labor, etc.) can be included as appropriate. The mechanism is designed to enable review (i.e., deep analysis, using rigorous audit and evaluation methods) of nontraditional audit areas such as organizational strategy, planning, procurement method, governance, project management, construction management, commissioning and start-up, closeout, creation of economic and social value, end-user satisfaction, whole-life costing, and more. This substantive approach to establishing a review allows the consultant a fuller understanding of the entity being reviewed and allows for arriving at more valuable recommendations and meaningful findings.

Such a comprehensive approach to performance review enables the client and/or consultant to tailor the review to stakeholder sensitivities, including any activity that potentially poses a material (substantial) risk and macrostrategic issues. It also enables the flexibility to review along the life cycle of the project, choosing different elements from the modular performance review concept that are applicable and meaningful at each stage of the project and scoping the review appropriately such that these elements can be targeted and reviewed in an appropriately in-depth fashion with a proactive and preventative approach instead of a reactive mindset. Economy and optimization of the project become the focus along with stewardship in the use of resources, such that more can be achieved with the available means while achieving the same (or better) expectations and quality. This is the new definition of performance.

The well-versed reader will notice that this review model expounds on some elements from established project management disciplines, systems, and methodologies, enabling a 'best of the best' approach to project review. The modular review concept incorporates a number of best practices from total cost management (TCM,[1] by AACE International), especially Module 1 – Planning and Module 6 – Management Controls, largely due to the specific performance audit focus of *Economy*, *Efficiency*, and *Effectiveness*. Other elements of the model are similar to (and can be used side by side with) total quality management (TQM) and quality of information approaches to continuous improvement (such as Kaizen and Deming) and process management as they apply to both projects and organizations; business justification, an assurance stance, risk awareness, and flexibility of PRINCE2 (Projects in Controlled Environments); the quality focus of international meta-standards (the International Standards Organization, ISO); organizational consistency (Six Sigma); scenario planning; peer reviews; benchmarking; Front End Engineering Design (FEED); and value engineering.

While this modular performance review model may at first cursory glance look similar to that of a stage gate review, it serves a very different purpose because the focus is on what is essential to the mission and success of the project and how to improve both the project and the organization. When scoped appropriately by selecting specific modules, the project performance review can be used to supplement the stage gate review and other program management methodologies but does not replace any of them. The Nalewaik-Mills Performance Review Method also builds on concepts from more traditional performance audit approaches that originated in public administration performance measurement and financial management, such as compliance and whole-organization perspective in the COSO (the Committee of Sponsoring Organizations of the Treadway Commission) ERM (Enterprise Risk Management) Framework, business process risk management and ISO 31000 (Risk Management – Principles and Guidelines), SOX (the Sarbanes-Oxley Act), financial stewardship, and operational audits. The performance review methodology enables the consultant to utilize best practices from any relevant sources to employ critical questioning in a system of interdependent problems, with a focus on whether every policy, procedure, action, and decision truly benefits the project and organization.

Broadening the approach to performance review also expands the scope of accountability. The very definition of accountability includes concepts of responsibility, liability, and punishment, answering for actions (or inaction) and consequences. There are many different kinds of accountability: legal, political, professional, and personal to cite a few, each with its own liabilities and consequences. When a project does not perform as expected or promised, stakeholders typically seek to understand what happened, why it happened, and who was responsible (although not necessarily in that order). Fault finding and finger pointing are not unusual. When something is perceived to have gone wrong, a forensic audit may be commissioned to determine the root cause and involved parties, gathering necessary documentation for legal action. It is characteristically expected that someone (a person, department, or company) be held accountable for such occurrences as budget busts, delayed completion, product or equipment failure, errors, injuries, and deaths. That accountable someone is then expected to somehow remedy the situation or make it right through a form of compensation or penance.

This Nalewaik-Mills Performance Review Method encourages an iterative review cycle and assumes more than one review will be conducted during the life cycle of the project in order to capture process and behavioral improvement opportunities at key times during the project life cycle. For example, the project's early days are an ideal time to evaluate project governance and team structure; shortly thereafter, the project will benefit greatly from a review of change management. Major performance reviews should be conducted prior to the formal approval of the project. Additional performance reviews may be conducted at key milestones or at certain project percentages complete (e.g., at quartiles – 25%, 50%, 75%, 100%). The review will have the most impact early in the project life cycle, when controls and project management processes can be improved and management is proactive instead of reactive. Additional discussion about the appropriateness and timing of various review scopes is included in the descriptions of each review module later in this book.

The Nalewaik-Mills Performance Review Method is intended to follow a Deming cycle that is repetitive. However, as subsequent reviews are performed, the client should note that the number and type of review findings will evolve as the project progresses, because the iterative cycle should result in continual improvement when steps are taken to resolve the findings from previous reviews and feedback loops are enabled and utilized. The amount of questioned expenditures may decline and the type of expenditures questioned may change due to improvements in expenditure controls, improved change management, and project-related changes in spending behavior. The number of qualitative findings may likewise decline, or their nature may change significantly due to such occurrences as lessons learned, resolution of past audit findings, streamlined or tightened policies and procedures, team member turnover, and an increase in project management sophistication. As the project moves through the various phases of its life cycle, different kinds of issues will surface and become significant, and others will be resolved or become immaterial (less meaningful). Different review scopes and approaches (i.e., modules) may also become necessary as the justifications and need for review evolve.

Economy, efficiency, and effectiveness

Key to any definition of performance audit are three specific terms: *Economy*, *Efficiency*, and *Effectiveness*. Optimizing and maximizing all three of these elements improves organizational maturity. These concurrently simple yet sophisticated concepts are defined in the following three paragraphs. The three Es cannot be defined for a project without a thorough understanding of the project objectives, goals, constraints, requirements, nature, mission, vision, and other pertinent aspects. The eight modules of the project performance review methodology are specifically designed to relate (directly or indirectly) to the three Es of performance and the performance review. Every single performance review activity should be conducted with these concepts in mind.

Economy

Economy is related to the minimization of inputs, project inputs being resources as explained earlier. The use of any or all resources may be reviewed for appropriateness, reasonability, careful management, prudence, and thriftiness. But the concept of *Economy* can also be reviewed in greater depth for a project performance review. The notion of *Economy* is especially important when compliance is part of the performance review; it recognizes that transactions may be formally and appropriately authorized but may still be willfully and knowingly unnecessary or excessive. Mere compliance does not suffice. In a project performance review, this could include a review of the procurement process (procurement method, purchase orders, and contracts) for achievement of objectives without overpayment. A benchmarked determination of price might be used for comparison to actual expenditures and unit rates. Whole-life cost, time, change, and risk management are also elements of *Economy*; a project (possibly procured through a low bid process) that experiences many change orders or costs the Owner more to operate and maintain can hardly be considered economic. An evaluation of *Economy* may also include a review of specifications to ensure project requirements are not higher than those necessary to produce desired results. These are just a few examples of how the concept of *Economy* can be reviewed in a project performance review.

Efficiency

Efficiency focuses on the optimal use (stewardship) of resources and reduction of waste. In a project review, value engineering (producing the same or better results for an approximate or reduced cost) during the design phase would be taken into consideration, along with a review of any gaps or overlaps in systems, technology, and staffing. Rightsizing (optimizing) a project, piece of equipment, or even a report can be considered a type of efficiency. Another area for review requiring specialty expertise is evaluation of *Efficiency* in practice (such as labor hours expended, materials/tools used or wasted, equipment hours, etc.) during the actual performance of the project. Productivity, schedule acceleration, and competency are other types of *Efficiency*, accomplishing a job with an appropriate expenditure of time and effort. While *Economy* and *Efficiency* may sometimes be difficult to distinguish from each other, they serve different purposes. *Economy* is about low cost, and *Efficiency* is about less waste.

Effectiveness

Effectiveness is a measure of the degree to which an activity (such as a project) produces a desired result and achieves an intended or expected outcome. Assessment of *Effectiveness* can be tricky, as it depends heavily on stakeholder definitions of success, value, and benefit. Measuring *Effectiveness* on projects requires a thorough understanding of the various stakeholder groups (including their situation, motives, interrelationships, power, and degree of influence) and a clear definition of project and organizational mission, vision, goals, and objectives. Review of *Effectiveness* also requires careful assessment of management practices, governance, and policies and procedures, which shape human behavior on projects.

The project life cycle

Although there are eight modules included in the method, there will likely not be a need to utilize all eight modules in the project performance review scope at any given time. This modular method provides the flexibility to add review elements or reexamine review elements during subsequent reviews conducted at a later date, as needed. The method is intended to be tailored to the specific needs of the project during key phases of the project life cycle. This means that different elements may be reviewed during different reviews, or some elements may appear in multiple reviews. The process is intended to be iterative, with the review repeated (and re-scoped) as appropriate, because performance is evolutionary, a continuous process that ebbs and flows. The descriptions of each module are intended to be a guide, not a checklist. If something isn't specifically mentioned, it can be added in any module where appropriate, especially specific concerns that are already known but need to be investigated or validated. If something is mentioned in one module but justification can be made for it to fit in a different module, the reviewers have the flexibility to scope the modules as best fits the review. The character and needs of the project change over time, and the performance review function needs to be responsive to that.

Apart from recovered costs, the primary benefit of performance review is gaining a 360-degree view of the project and developing findings that can address behavior while the project is still underway, thus both understanding and improving project and organizational performance. The modules enable a review that can be targeted to specific concerns as appropriate at particular times during the project life cycle. Importantly, longitudinal study of a project provides data in context and enables the reviewer to give a more comprehensive report on performance and evolution over time. One project review is not enough to provide a complete perspective on and forecast of project behavior, except when performed retrospectively as a project closeout review. As part of a lessons-learned program, the findings from project reviews can be used in the development of future projects.

Projects have a discrete beginning and an end, because by their own definition they are temporary organizations. During its life cycle, a project goes through several distinct phases and reaches key milestones. Although any module can be reviewed at any time during the project, Figure 3.1 illustrates which modules are likely most relevant during four key phases of the project life cycle.

INITIATION	DEVELOPMENT	EXECUTION and CONTROLLING	CLOSEOUT
1 - Planning	1 - Planning	2 - Stakeholders	3 - Risk
4 - Compliance	2 - Stakeholders	3 - Risk	4 - Compliance
5 - Resources	3 - Risk	4 - Compliance	7 - Post-Project Concerns
8 - Special Issues	4 - Compliance	5 - Resources	8 - Special Issues
	5 - Resources	6 - Management Controls	
	6 - Management Controls	8 - Special Issues	
	8 - Special Issues		

Figure 3.1 Module relevance to project life cycle phases

During the project Initiation phase, the idea of the project is conceived or triggered in the context of organizational strategic objectives, and performance requirements (definitions of success) are determined. Module 1 – Planning is important because it addresses the challenges of matching project objectives with long-term strategy. In the Initiation phase, other modules can also be applied. Module 4 – Compliance applies to organizational policies and procedures and legislative and regulatory requirements that are relevant during the early phases of the project. Module 5 – Resources is pertinent in the context of project funding and resource planning. There may be other issues that require targeted review, which may be addressed in Module 8 – Special Issues.

The project Development phase has as its deliverable a completely developed project plan that can be used during the Execution and Controlling phase. During this phase, a roadmap is developed for the use and investment of resources to deliver the project. A key deliverable for this phase is formal approval from a board of directors or senior management for the go-ahead of the project and release of funds for project use. Some activities undertaken during the Development phase may overlap with or refine work done during the Initiation phase and project approvals, depending on the organization. Based on the importance of this phase, almost all project performance audit modules will be utilized. During the project Development phase, stakeholder input and definitions of success are paramount (Module 2 – Stakeholders), along with risk assessment (Module 3 – Risk) and the development and implementation of governance (Module 6 – Management Controls). Module 1 – Planning, Module 4 – Compliance, Module 5 – Resources, and Module 8 – Special Issues may continue to be meaningful during this project phase.

During the project Execution and Controlling phase, project plans are implemented and project activities conducted in accordance with the plan, specifications, and requirements. The project becomes very dynamic. Compliance (Module 4 – Compliance) becomes even more important and evolves to focus on compliance with processes, policies and procedures, statutory and regulatory requirements, and purchase orders and contracts. The Execution and Controlling phase is governed by project management methodologies, project controls, and internal controls, as addressed in Module 6 – Management Controls; change management is especially important at this time. Engagement with stakeholders (Module 2 – Stakeholders), careful management of resources (Module 5 – Resources), and risk management (Module 3 – Risk) remain as ongoing efforts during this project phase, evolving to be rapidly responsive to changing project conditions. As with the previous phases, Module 8 – Special Issues is used as a catch-all for any other issues that require targeted review.

At project Closeout, the project is delivered after having shown it performs according to the defined requirements. The project will result in an asset or deliverable that serves some purpose. The project Closeout phase requires testing and verification of performance, generating information and documentation to be used in operations and maintenance phases of the asset life cycle. There will be certain requirements that need to be satisfied in order for project closeout to occur (Module 4 – Compliance), and specific concerns regarding the closeout process, final accounting, and the transition to the product or asset life cycle (Module 7 – Post-Project Concerns). Historic data and lessons learned will be gathered with respect to risk (Module 3 – Risk), the use of resources (Module 5 – Resources), and more (Module 8 – Special Issues).

Note

1 Technical Board. (2006). *Total Cost Management Framework*. Morgantown, WV: AACE International.

4 Overview of the Nalewaik-Mills Performance Review Method

Module 1 – Planning

The success or failure of the project begins before the project really exists, when it is an idea that still needs to be formed, funded, approved, and planned. Project approvals depend on whether or not a project is well-presented for consideration, and there may be more than one project competing for available funding. This module focuses on the process of creating the project, matching project objectives with long-term strategy, and developing a plan for the project to follow.

During the initiation phase of the project, the Owner identifies projects that are necessary in order to satisfy enterprise business strategy, and objectives. Strategic planning, master planning, benchmarking, selection and prioritization of projects, and other activities will be conducted and taken into consideration. Stakeholder requirements are an important part of the initiation phase of the project, and planning requires stakeholder analysis as addressed in Module 2 – Stakeholders. Well-crafted stakeholder requirements and the rationale for creating the project, can both serve as bases of performance measurement. Up to this point, the organization's effort focuses on identifying what is desired or what needs to be accomplished, and justifying the effort.

The next step in creating the project focuses on how best to achieve (or, if the requirements or specifications are unachievable, approximate) the desired result. The project team and consultants use the project definition (goal), constraints, and various types of requirements (user, business, performance, regulatory, etc.) to develop and evaluate various execution strategies and approaches for realizing the project and choose the best fit. Each execution strategy option will have its benefits and challenges and will require allocation of resources; investment decision making and economic evaluation of the whole-life project cost are examples of processes that are typically part of this effort. Execution strategy often focuses on the project

Nalewaik-Mills Performance Review Method

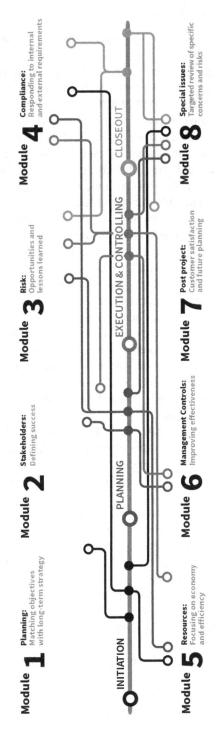

Module **1** Planning:
Matching objectives
with long-term strategy

Module **2** Stakeholders:
Defining success

Module **3** Risk:
Opportunities and
lessons learned

Module **4** Compliance:
Responding to internal
and external requirements

Module **5** Resources:
Focusing on economy
and efficiency

Module **6** Management Controls:
Improving effectiveness

Module **7** Post project:
Customer satisfaction
and future planning

Module **8** Special issues:
Targeted review of specific
concerns and risks

INITIATION   PLANNING   EXECUTION & CONTROLLING   CLOSEOUT

Figure 4.1 Nalewaik-Mills Performance Review Method

performance objectives of *Economy* and *Efficiency*, tied closely to concepts of value.

Once the basics of the project scope have been established during the initiation phase and deliverables defined, design/engineering and implementation planning processes will commence in the development phase, including creation of scenario-specific estimates and schedules, development and approval of budgets, establishment of cost and schedule baselines, identification of funding sources, resource requirements, cost of quality, and value engineering. There will likely be several iterations of these, including peer reviews and additional economic analysis regarding investment return, as the project plan is fine-tuned and more definition and refinement are enabled. The focus on *Economy* and *Efficiency* continues along with evaluations of different scenarios for ultimate value and utility. If time to market is a priority, the planning effort will concentrate on streamlining processes, material receipt, and contractor coordination in order to accelerate projects. Once design and engineering are completed, procurement decisions will be made regarding the contract and delivery mechanism that best suit the project. Depending on the organization, there may be considerable overlap between and intermingling of these several project phases.

Risk analysis is an important part of the initiation and planning processes and requires close attention both at this point in time and also throughout the project life cycle, as addressed in Module 3 – Risk. Resource analysis is likewise conducted at this time and throughout the project, as addressed in Module 5 – Resources.

The purpose of Module 1 – Planning is to provide assurance to stakeholders regarding the solidity of justification for decisions made during the initiation, planning, development, design/engineering, and procurement processes on the project. The objective is to confirm that the project was planned for success – that is, able to meet the organization's strategic objectives and requirements as defined by stakeholders. However, the future is unknown, and almost nothing happens exactly according to plan. This is where the performance review adds value, by trying to identify how or why the project might not achieve its performance goals. The reviewer achieves this by reviewing the documents against which project success will be measured, such as the project charter, business case, project execution plan, basis of design, and so forth.

The performance review is intended to review any elements of the project that might impact project performance. As the project requirements define performance, a critical review of project requirements may be inappropriate for a performance review. If there are questions about or issues with project requirements, specifications, design, engineering, and the like, those will likely be addressed as part of a forensic audit or technical review. A later chapter in this book discusses elements to exclude from the performance review and conduct separately.

A key area for concern is the project budget. The reviewer should be able to find supporting documentation for the development of the project budget for project acceptance. If documentation is missing, especially signature approvals or board authorizations, this may be an indication of abuse of authority, noncompliance with procedures, or a lack of informed decision making. While lack of documentation might not impact project performance per se, it would be an issue to report here or in Module 4 – Compliance. The reviewers should also be able to readily obtain and review supporting documentation justifying evolution of the project budget or scope. Again, missing documentation should be reported. However, the reviewer's role should go farther than just reporting missing documentation; at all times, the reviewer should critically question such deficiencies and be proactive in seeking out behavior that potentially puts project success at risk.

Project cost overruns may occur as a result of the politics of project approval, where the project cost is initially understated (and return on investment [ROI] overstated) in order to get the project accepted. Some project overruns may occur as a result of excessive stakeholder influence; for example, stakeholders that withhold required funding, signatures, or permits until additional items of scope are added to the project. In such a situation, there may be a lack of supporting documentation to justify decisions and assumptions made regarding the project planning and approvals. Lack of documentation is a warning sign that the investment decision-making process was somehow compromised and should prompt the reviewer to investigate more deeply in this module and related modules such as Module 2 – Stakeholders and Module 6 – Management Controls.

The auditor should also be keenly aware of other issues, such as budget anchoring, wherein the project budget fails to evolve and adjust to the reality of the project. In other words, the project team becomes so attached to the original value of the budget that they refuse to adjust it even while recognizing key elements of the project (such as scope) have fundamentally changed. In fact, throughout the project, performance problems can occur any time there is rigid adherence to anything as immutable truths.

Other elements of project initiation, planning, development, design/engineering, and procurement that can be considered during a performance review are any that may impact project performance or offer clues regarding project performance. For example:

- Late-in-the-project changes that result from changes in business strategy and objectives

- Failure to meet performance expectations and needs when scope and design suffer as a result of a gap between project needs and available funding
- Project performance issues related to the documentation and communication of requirements
- Financial opportunities that are time sensitive or have deadlines, including matching and reimbursable funds
- Review and improvement of contract terms
- Unrealistic cash flow projections
- Delivery method, contracting, and/or procurement mechanisms and processes that impact the project cost or schedule
- Changes to the delivery method or contract in the middle of the project and the consequences or improvements that result
- Schedule milestones and end dates that are based on an organizational anniversary or other deadline, forcing an unrealistic critical path

As with the other project performance modules, it is up to the reviewer to listen to client concerns and use interviews and available project documentation to identify and target elements in this module to be reviewed. These examples are only a small handful of issues that may be reviewed related to project initiation, planning, design/engineering, and procurement.

Module 2 – Stakeholders

Key to concepts of success, failure, and value are the many project stakeholders and their level of involvement with the project and organization. Because success is a highly subjective topic, definitions and measurement of success will vary diversely depending on the stakeholder. In fact, when one considers all internal, external, direct, and indirect stakeholders, it is likely that there will be conflicting definitions of success. It's not uncommon for a project or element of a project to be simultaneously a success and a failure, as defined by different stakeholders. Stakeholders have considerable impact in the project performance concept of *Effectiveness*; of the three Es, the notion of *Effectiveness* is almost as subjective and contentious as definitions of success, which makes it the most difficult to review. As mentioned earlier, because success is part of the very definition of project performance, and stakeholder requirements are a key element in the inception and planning of a project, this module is closely related to Module 1.

This module is intended to help the client and review team consider the various types of stakeholders on the project (individuals, formalized groups, and entities/companies) and their many different levels of interest, power, and influence held at various times during the project. Essentially, the review and project teams need to know their intended audiences and address them accordingly during both the project and the project review. Failure to understand and manage stakeholders could very well mean failure of the project. During a performance review, failure to understand stakeholders might mean a failure to appropriately scope the review, resulting in an audit expectations gap.

The list of project stakeholders can be seemingly infinite. Their relationship with and investment in the project may be contractual, social, emotional, financial, familial, political, and more. They can be grouped as internal or external, explicit or implicit, and upstream or downstream to the project. The list of stakeholders may include companies and their employees, contractors/vendors/suppliers, consultants, neighbors, creditors/investors, partners, end users, elected officials, governing bodies (including government) and regulatory agencies, the general public, industry groups and unions, special interest groups, and even future generations. It may even include media and activist organizations that purport to behave in the best interest of stakeholders.

It isn't enough to just list and categorize stakeholders. Identifying stakeholders also means knowing their concerns, comprehending how they define success and value, understanding their motivations (such as profit, power, and achievement), gaining insight into how much they understand of the

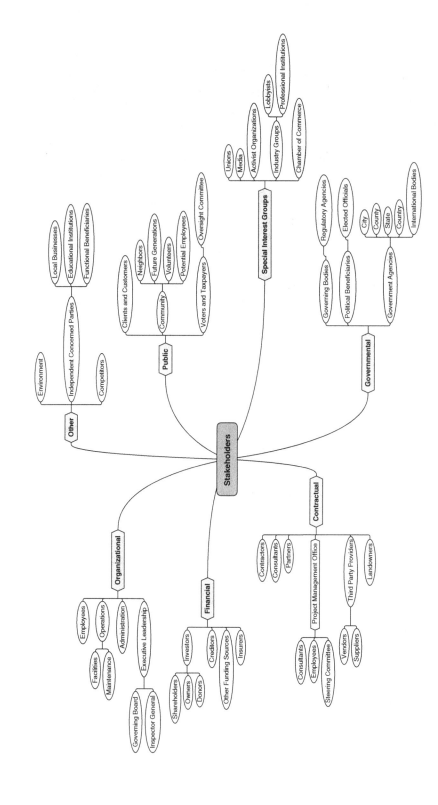

project, and quantifying their level of tolerance for risk and change. It also means understanding how much power and influence is held by specific stakeholder groups and how they can cause changes to scope, procurement, and other areas of the project, impacting project *Economy* and *Efficiency* (and thus performance).

The reviewers should be able to obtain the preliminary stakeholder list developed when defining user and other requirements for the project, during the initiation phase, including the ranking and prioritization of stakeholders according to legitimacy, urgency, power, and influence. This documentation, if available, could be reviewed during the performance review to develop an understanding of the stakeholders and project environment and thus their expectations of the review. For the purposes of this exercise, deep investigation should be limited to those stakeholders who can significantly impact project performance.

Stakeholder identification is not a one-time exercise during the project; stakeholders depart, new stakeholders arrive, and stakeholder effects on the project ebb and flow throughout the project life cycle. Stakeholder beliefs and motivations can change. This is why reeducation of stakeholders regarding project concepts, processes, terminology, and history is a never-ending (and sometimes frustrating) cycle during the project. The reviewer should look for evidence that an iterative approach has been taken by the project team regarding stakeholder identification and related communication plans.

Working with and managing stakeholders also means developing shared language and innovative mechanisms for ease of communication. Stakeholder ability will vary regarding their capacity to communicate needs and wants. If stakeholders cannot adequately communicate their needs or understand project documentation, the project may be accidentally designed to inappropriate requirements. Stakeholders may need certain kinds of data but might not even know what words to use when asking for it. Some stakeholders cannot understand project design drawings and may be better served by 3-D physical or virtual representations of the project product. These are only a few examples of how project communications need to be specifically tailored to the audience. The reviewer can look for evidence that the project team has taken steps to understand the context of language used by stakeholders and stakeholder abilities to comprehend and convey technical concepts.

The project team also needs to be acutely aware that, in many cases, stakeholders' (especially public stakeholders') understanding of the projected project outcome, real-world appearance, and timeline for delivery are mismatched with reality, leading to unachievable expectations and unnecessary criticism (which, with public stakeholders, results in very bad press). Stakeholders rely on the project team to provide them with information on project status. This module presents an opportunity for the reviewer to review communication matrices and plans specific to each stakeholder group for content, level of depth, timing, and simplicity of language that meet both stakeholder and organizational needs.

Formal oversight bodies such as a board of directors, steering committee, citizen oversight committee, project sponsor/executive, or audit committee are both governance mechanisms and stakeholders. The typical function of such groups is to enact legislative- or regulatory-required supervision, monitor progress, and provide support and guidance to project leadership with a certain level of authority and area of responsibility. They will typically have an agreed-upon charter. A steering committee or other executive-level body may be the higher authority in situations in which decision making, problem solving, and issue resolution have been unsuccessful at the project level. While not necessarily directly responsible for managing the project, an oversight body sets the overall tone of the project, needs to recognize the strategic implications and outcomes of project initiatives, requires a broad understanding of project management and risk, and receives appropriate information for both decision making and reporting to their own stakeholders. During the performance review, processes may be mapped to identify gaps and overlaps in oversight and communication and assess whether the oversight bodies are able to fulfill their role or mandate. For instance, does the project team merely report to the oversight body, or does the oversight body actually make decisions? Reporting to oversight bodies should be considered during the performance review for such issues as timeliness, accuracy, *Effectiveness*, content, and appropriateness. Different committees or boards will need to receive different kinds of reports with different information; there might not be a one-size-fits-all solution to the report format. Review of the role and *Effectiveness* of formal oversight bodies and reporting to such bodies may overlap with elements of performance review in Module 6 – Management Controls.

Additional stakeholder-related items and activities can be considered during a performance review, specifically those that may impact project performance or offer clues regarding project performance. For example:

- Mismatches among current project performance, definitions of success, and concepts of value
- Absence of mechanisms for establishing and managing expectations
- Stakeholder levels of tolerance for risk and change
- Stakeholder interdependencies, which compound stakeholder impact
- Inappropriate influence by stakeholders and unchecked power
- Stakeholder accountability and responsibilities
- Conflict between stakeholders and issues of stakeholder equity

- Stakeholder turnover in the middle of the project, impacting project requirements and perception of success
- Managing the stakeholder general public
- Managing the media

These examples are only a handful of ways that stakeholders can influence a project and mechanisms for managing their expectations. It is the client's responsibility to share as much information as possible with the reviewers regarding project stakeholders, and part of the reviewer's due diligence includes comprehending the stakeholder base and context of the project.

Module 3 – Risk

One of the objectives of the performance review is to identify both project and enterprise vulnerabilities and opportunities and develop findings intended to strengthen related controls. Therefore risk assessment is a key element of the performance review. Risk has many definitions and is treated in many ways at the organizational level. The authors, too often, have been referred to the insurance department when they inquired about project risk management. Risk can be a confusing concept. For the purposes of this book, risk in the context of projects is the chance or hazard of a loss, often commercial. Risk and opportunity analysis focuses on the project's likelihood of achieving its objectives; systemic risks are barriers to project performance, and opportunities (when realized) can improve project performance. These are, in the real world, a natural consequence of undertaking any activity or endeavor due to inherent uncertainty. Risk and opportunity exist, always. They are multifaceted and interdependent and constantly changing. Any action has more than one possible outcome and impact, and any action (or lack thereof) may affect existing risks or generate subsequent ones. Every action and inaction on a project has an impact, a type of project butterfly effect. Avoiding a project instead of undertaking it is not necessarily a way to avoid all risk; indeed, failure to act carries risks of its own.

Because one of the objectives of the performance review is to understand both project and enterprise vulnerabilities and opportunities and develop findings intended to strengthen related controls, examination of risk assessment is a key element of the performance review. Risk assessment may be a statutory requirement, and executive-level stakeholders are, increasingly, keenly aware of systemic risks and risk management efforts. In project management, risk awareness and treatment are a key element of good governance, and they are a recurring/iterative exercise. The review process itself can be interpreted as a supplement to step three (check) and precursor to step four (adjust) of the Deming cycle (plan, do, check, adjust) that is typical of risk management. The review will not supplant formal risk assessment and management methods, but it can be used to supplement them and consider their level of completeness, robustness, and reasonableness of conclusions.

Risk assessment tries to identify ways in which a project is likely to experience debilitating issues, failure, or change. As such, it can be structured to perform as an early warning system. A formal risk management process includes identifying systemic risks and developing a list, often through historic data, a workshop, and interviews. This will include inherent risks that are faced by the organization as part of the very nature of its activities and for which there should be existing policies and procedures. Risks can be objective or subjective and may be unknown then become known at a later date. Most organizations will rank identified risks according to priority based on level of perceived threat or severity and consequences as they related to project and corporate objectives.

Risk assessment requires objective professional judgment, but experts are difficult to normalize and calibrate. So-called expert opinion may be one of the most unreliable parts of the risk assessment; there is no guarantee that numbers provided are thoroughly thought out and documented. The expert's opinion may be subjective or based on an undocumented 'gut feeling'. The expert may have a higher tolerance for risk than the rest of the project team and executive. Risk tolerance is how we justify making decisions and then acting with overconfidence on what we think we know.

Risks can be grouped into a number of categories, shown in what follows with examples of typical events that may generate a true risk. The categories below are somewhat typical in practice but will vary in subtle ways, and some of the examples may be fluid among several categories. The reviewer's role is to ensure the risk assessment has considered the wide range of risks and opportunities potentially associated with the project and that those risks and opportunities have been properly identified and quantified.

Some organizations will take the additional step of using Monte Carlo–type techniques to quantify them in terms of probability and impact and develop a model that can be used to calculate necessary contingency and float. Quantification of systemic risks tends not to focus on extreme-impact (project-killing) statistically unlikely events such as war, terrorism, political instability, corruption, earthquakes, tsunami, stock market crash, extreme operational risks of the type discussed in Basel II (et seq.), space alien invasion, zombie apocalypse, and so on. While these might not be modeled or quantified, they should not be ignored. Risks modeled are project specific, and some may be related to the organization. One of the challenges with risk modeling is overconfidence that things are perfectly predictable, resulting in overreliance on the model. The authors are aware of a fairly recent client trend away from sophisticated risk modeling, which has resulted from client realization that hands-on management and mitigation of risk offer more value to them than infinitely precise quantification.

As with project planning, all assumptions regarding risk assessment should be carefully documented, especially where risk analysis is used to determine monetary contingency and other measures of protection. In-depth risk analysis may help the project team decide how best to avoid, reduce, or transfer systemic risks or may even result in a decision to accept certain risks as is. Opportunities may be exploited, shared, enhanced, or accepted. Key to a structured risk management process is documenting not just the

Technical Risks
- proven/unproven technology
- new product development
- implementation methodology
- equipment and material performance
- planning and design complexity
- commissioning and testing
- evolving requirements
- tie-in to existing project or interface
- scope change
- engineering and design change
- metric vs. imperial measurement
- differing standards
- specialized equipment and materials
- long-lead equipment
- project in an operating facility
- design conflict/interference
- information systems
- scalability
- security vulnerabilities
- technical complexity

Financial and Economic Risks
- inflation
- funding/financing
- market forces
- bidder perception of risk
- labor and material costs and drivers
- labor and material availability
- interest rate
- currency fluctuation
- bankruptcy
- alternative approaches to insurance

Contractual Risks
- contractual liability
- warranties
- liquidated/consequential/punitive damages
- construction defect
- risk transfer
- conflicting contract language
- inadequate contract protections
- intellectual property
- new contract/delivery method

Statutory and Political Risks
- local law or government policy
- government influence on disputes
- environmental regulations
- property acquisition
- permitting
- external stakeholder influence
- testing and certification
- official and unofficial holidays
- religious observance
- customs (import/export)
- visas (immigration)

Organizational Risks
- project team capability
- contractor failure
- contractor/vendor/consultant failure or default
- mergers and acquisitions
- staff turnover
- stakeholder turnover
- degree of unfamiliarity
- schedule acceleration
- gaps in responsibility or scope
- communication
- executive support of project
- business processes
- delegated authority
- organizational culture
- reputation

Other Risks
- climate
- safety
- unknown conditions
- archaeological findings
- contamination
- local customs
- infrastructure
- theft
- translation error
- productivity
- competition

Figure 4.3 Types of risk

risk but also the treatment plan and continuously monitoring the risk. The risk management plan should include a description of the risk, likelihood of occurrence, potential impact, consequences, risk owners, root causes, triggers, early warning signs, and treatment or action plan. A sample risk management form is shown in Figure 4.3.

Management of risk is an iterative process. Project risks are dynamic, not static, with new risks developing and residual risks changing over time. Repeating the risk management process means identifying new risks, closing risks that no longer exist, and monitoring and requantifying already-known risks. As mentioned earlier, because risk is a key element in the inception and planning of a project, this module is closely related to Module 1 – Planning, but it is included as a separate module because it is relevant throughout the project life cycle.

Risk management is often conducted as a discrete project exercise, but the review scope and reviewer also benefit from an understanding of the risks unique to the project and the organization. Reviewers should be able to obtain and review supporting documentation for the risk management process. Reviewing an existing list of project risks and risk management plans allows reviewers to identify crucial functions and understand how risk tolerance varies from a stakeholder perspective. Using known risks to assist in developing the scope of the review allows a focus of review resources on those areas of the project that present high risk, are critical to performance, or otherwise represent an opportunity for review findings and organizational improvement. Risks can have considerable impact on project *Economy* and *Effectiveness*, possibly less impact on *Efficiency*. When expenditure testing is part of the review, the scope may include testing a greater percentage of expenditures in high-risk areas. Findings from the performance review may even result in the identification of additional areas of systemic risk that can be added to the risk assessment and management plan.

Although understanding of risk is most applicable in the performance review as a mechanism for targeting the audit scope, any risk elements can be reviewed during a performance review and also the risk management process itself. For example:

- Use of appropriate contract language to transfer risk
- Purchase of insurance to offset risk
- Selection of delivery method to transfer and reduce risk
- Failure to monitor, manage, and resolve risks
- Failure to conduct risk modeling if required (may be a statutory or regulatory requirement)
- Existence of a hotline, Inspector General office, or other provisions for the reporting and investigation of fraud

Risk Entry Form

Risk #: _____

Date : _____
Risk Owner : _____

Risk Description	
Consequence	
Current Mitigation	
Notes Field	
Fallback Plan	

	Impact
Probability	
Time Impact	
Cost Impact	
Business Impact?	

Risk Reduction Measures

Action #:	Action Manager	Description	Target Date	Actual Date	Status
1					
2					
3					
4					

Figure 4.4 Risk management form

- Understatement of risk
- Risks related to newness and change
- Communication of risk to stakeholders
- QA/QC of the risk program

Part of the reviewer's due diligence includes comprehending project risk and conducting the review with risk and opportunity at the forefront of the performance equation. Risk analysis and treatment are key modules in performance improvement.

Module 4 – Compliance

Although the primary focus of the Nalewaik-Mills Performance Review Method is on assurance, compliance is also important. The compliance module of a review is, simply put, a review of adherence to certain mandatory requirements, contract terms, laws, guidelines, policies and procedures, or rules. These mandatory requirements are also known as audit criteria. Compliance can sometimes be used as a proxy for accountability.

The concept of compliance is so entrenched in management and in audit culture that it appears pervasively in most audit and review scopes (not just in performance review). Indeed, consultants tend to promise high returns from contract compliance reviews, with some clients relying on recovered expenditures (such as unallowable costs and duplicate payments) to offset the cost of the review. The discipline of compliance auditing is well established, with comprehensive methodologies and standards that apply.

Although a compliance review may be conducted separately from the performance review, a compliance module is appropriate to include in performance review scope because compliance may be a factor in stakeholder definitions of performance and success. If compliance review is part of the scope of the performance review, relevant audit standards may apply. Clients almost always request some element of compliance within the performance review scope, and there may be a regulatory, funding source, or corporate governance requirement for the inclusion of compliance review. Several types of compliance testing are most common: regulatory, funding requirements, contracts/expenditures, and policies and procedures.

Regulatory compliance reviews project activities in the context of mandatory applicable laws, codes, standards, and regulatory/statutory requirements, often from an external agency or authority. Regulations may also be self-imposed by an organization. Issues identified during regulatory compliance review may result in controls improvements on projects (such as the use of checklists at closeout or for other activities) to ensure regulatory requirements are always satisfied.

Funding requirements analysis considers expenditures as they are governed by the terms and conditions of funding sources. Funding sources may be public funds generated through taxes or bonds, matching funds, loans, subsidies, crowdfunding, or perhaps a grant or donation from a specific public or private entity. Expenditures of restricted funds are constrained to specific purposes or timing and can be audited for compliance with those deadlines and conditions, whereas unrestricted funds may be used in any way. Typical findings include coding to the wrong funding source, inappropriate use of funds, lack of justification for utilization of the funding source, and expenditures that exceed the funding amount or were spent after a deadline had passed. Funding requirements compliance review promotes accountability and transparency to the entities providing the funding and, in the case of public funds, the general public.

With contract/expenditure testing, invoices are sampled and reviewed for accuracy and supporting documentation and appropriateness to the project. They are also typically reviewed for compliance with budget, contract, and purchase order terms (such as: contractual maximums regarding expenditures and change orders, unit rates, allowable labor burden, and nonreimbursable costs). The review may include an assessment of reasonability for such things as item cost, unit rates, and overhead; while not specifically a compliance exercise, it is an audit common practice and does add value to the performance review mandate of reviewing unnecessary or overspending and thus *Economy*. Change orders may be included in this type of contract and expenditure testing. Typical findings include unallowable or duplicate charges, missing documentation, overcharges, incorrect rates, math errors, and coding errors. Correcting errors may include recovering funds from appropriate parties, using either the contract or legal means as remedy. However, recovery is not always possible, or an executive-level decision may be made that recovery is not prudent. The authors recall an instance in which the Owner valued the relationship with the contractor more than the millions of monies spent in error because they had dire need of the contractor and their subcontractors for an extremely large future project. In such instances, the reviewer should obtain justification and evidence of approvals for such decision making.

Contract compliance is not necessarily limited to just expenditures. A review of compliance with a contract may also include compliance with contract terms regarding administration of the contract or approval of invoices. For example, the contract may require certain documentation always be provided with the contractor's monthly invoice, such as the current project schedule and a status report. If any of this information is missing, yet the invoice is paid, the reviewer should obtain justification and evidence of approvals for the circumvention of contract requirements.

A review of compliance with policies and procedures and other governance mechanisms (as discussed in Module 6 – Management Controls) may include many types of processes, such as security policies, user access controls, expenditure controls, change controls, documentation requirements, risk management, project management, project controls, and the like. In such a review, the consultant evaluates the capability of the management systems and governance mechanisms to ensure compliance. If it is discovered that policies and procedures are not being followed, a determination needs to be made regarding whether the omission is accidental or intentional. Sometimes deliberate noncompliance can be an indication that processes are cumbersome, unnecessary, or duplicative and can be improved in some manner. Examples of improvements to processes include empowering individuals to make decisions; revising or pooling existing assets, resources, and systems; streamlining and automating processes; institutionalizing processes; improving *Efficiency*; and redeploying staff resources. Policies and procedures compliance review contributes to good governance and improvements to governance mechanisms.

One of the challenges with compliance review is that fault finding and reporting on exceptions, which often are the result of human error, may be counterproductive to the intent of a performance review. Part of this tone is set by the organization; a review with intent to penalize will yield precisely that and very little else. However, this penalty approach is not typically conducive to organizational learning and positive change. Materiality (data and substance) must be considered, lest the compliance review unnecessarily focus stakeholder attention on trivial mistakes instead of broader performance problems that need to be remedied. However, in the specific cases of regulatory and funding compliance, violations are a serious matter and may result in severe penalties.

The findings from compliance review may result in:

- Changes to policies and procedures
- Training of staff, stakeholders, and team members
- Penalties and fines
- Improved expenditure controls
- Improved internal controls
- Improved change controls
- Questioned, rejected, and recovered expenditures
- Reallocated expenditures and recoding
- Strengthened contract and purchase order language
- Legal interpretations of regulatory and funding requirements

These are just a few examples of types of compliance review and potential impact from findings. When developing the performance review scope, the auditor needs to identify and understand any compliance frameworks that exist on the project and review project activities and expenditures accordingly.

Module 5 – Resources

The very definitions of *Economy*, *Efficiency*, and *Effectiveness* focus on the utilization of resources as inputs; the best and most appropriate use of resources is at the very heart of performance review. Using this project performance review method, the concept of resources becomes broadened beyond the typical audit focus of cost and internal controls. Resources that can be reviewed during a performance review are any that may impact project success, and the methods of evaluation (quantitative or qualitative) will need to be tailored to the specific type of resource and available data.

The first step of the resource analysis module involves the identification of resources to be assessed. Typical project resources include money, time, people, materials, consumables, equipment, information, and more. On any project, program, or portfolio, there are plenty of types of resources to review but likely not nearly enough time to review them all. Once project resources are identified, tied to risks, and prioritized, the auditor can select the project resources to review and use available data and interviews to identify overlaps, overburdening, gaps in available resources, and other opportunities for addition, subtraction, reallocation, and streamlining of resources. Resources may be analyzed at the project level, program/portfolio level, or activity level.

Resources might not be unique to a project; on a program or portfolio, they may be shared across projects. In such instances, the reviewer should ensure cost and time charges to projects are accurate and appropriate. The reviewer can also work with the project team to seek best alternative uses for resources and make recommendations accordingly.

Lack of a resource can be seen as a project constraint that can severely affect performance, whereas excess use of resources should be treated as waste. The concept of waste may be considered in several ways, including material waste, labor productivity, time, consumables waste (including tools), land utilization and valuation, utilities consumption, natural resource utilization, and building utilization.

Resource use is related to project schedule in that time is a resource and any delay in the provision or availability of other resources may cause a delay to the project or even a failure to deliver. As such, resource analysis may include identifying resource bottlenecks and constraints, criticality, long-lead items, and scheduled replenishment/renewal of stored items. Vendor, supplier, contractor, and subcontractor capacity may be an issue. Some of these problems may be solved by identifying opportunities for streamlining, automation, added shifts, and outsourcing. Review of the schedule and the use of 4-D modeling may identify issues with resource loading, leveling, conflicts, supply chain, and activity sequencing.

Regarding the project team itself, resource review may identify overburdened project team members, unfilled roles, gaps, overlaps, competence, and issues with team member turnover. The auditor can use the organization chart and roles and responsibilities documentation to review the appropriateness of staffing. Solutions to project team problems may be achieved through outsourcing, on-call consultants, succession planning, reassignment of roles, compensation, and training/development.

Team member turnover may be indicative of organizational challenges and poor management or market conditions. Such turnover poses a risk to the project, because with the loss of staff comes loss of institutional knowledge and project/organizational history. Where there is team member turnover, the reviewer can look for succession planning, capture of project history and lessons learned, and interviews of outgoing staff, all of which may help mitigate the effect of losing existing staff and ease the process of onboarding new people.

Additional resources to review and related issues may include (but are not limited to):

- Underutilized knowledge, skills, and expertise (team member resumes)
- Duplication of or need for information systems and hardware
- Inventory and warehousing
- Materials management and receiving
- Equipment utilization, cost allocation, and fair market value
- Cash flow analysis, if not already evaluated in Module 1 – Planning
- Effective use of technology

Information from Module 3 – Risk may be used to prioritize resource analysis, and data from other modules (especially Module 1 – Planning) may also be applicable to the review. Module 6 – Management Controls is the next logical step in determining the control of and authority for use of project resources.

Module 6 – Management controls

Potentially the largest in scope of the review modules, the Management Controls module focuses on the review of project management, project controls, and related governance processes, policies, and procedures. This includes the softer side of governance and project management, such as culture, communication, and reporting.

In a review of project performance, cost management and quality assurance tend to draw the most focus; these two relate closely to concepts of *Economy* and *Effectiveness*. Other areas of management controls review will depend on the specific concerns and priorities of the organization and project. It may be easiest for the reviewers to break the management controls element of the project performance review into modules as defined by department or role, focusing first on critical functions and areas of risk as identified in Module 3 – Risk. Another approach is to structure the review according to the management controls required and deliverables expected at major milestones in the project life cycle.

Governance is the establishment and implementation of formal processes and informal constructs that guide management activity, creating constraints and implementing controls. Some of these mechanisms confer autonomy and decision-making authority on the part of the enterprise. Governance occurs at all levels of management and is the framework within which management functions; the governance of projects is influenced by the governance of the parent organization, and all of the above are affected by individuals' self-governance. Accountability, consistency, predictability, and transparency are elements of good governance, as is process *Efficiency*. Formal products of governance include contracts, policies and procedures, processes, rules and regulations, flowcharts, systems, organizational structure, codified decision-making processes, and project documentation, all of which can be reviewed in this module. At the other end of the spectrum are informal normative controls, which may include culture, internalized goals, values, trust, and other relational elements. Audits and reviews themselves are also a governance mechanism. Governance is about control and includes (but is not limited to) management controls, project controls, procurement controls, internal controls, systems controls, and financial controls. The review can focus on improving governance mechanisms such that they provide value, not just bureaucracy.

It is fairly rare for project and program management plans, policies and procedures, and other governance tools and products to be developed from scratch specifically for a project. More often, they are carried forward from previous projects or companies, with some adaptations to suit the requirements of the current project and/or Owner. Tools may be cobbled together from various disparate sources, integrating Owner-specific, project-specific, and best practice processes. The tools may include written procedures, forms and templates, software, computerized systems, and so on. On international projects, the variety of languages, units of measurement, laws, and cultures to incorporate into management controls is even more complex. The problem with trying to incorporate many needs and scale-up processes for large programs is that the governance tools may become convoluted, inappropriate, inconsistent in process or language, or even duplicative; care must be taken when assembling documentation from several sources.

During a performance review, written policies and procedures and program management plans can be reviewed for completeness, ease of use, reasonability, and consistency and processes mapped to facilitate the identification of improvement opportunities. The reviewer can look for opportunities to optimize and integrate work processes end to end through the project life cycle. The reviewer should be mindful that, when policies and procedures are widely overlooked or applied in a trivial manner, it may be indicative of an inappropriate process.

A key issue with management controls is avoiding material differences between organizational policies as designed and intended and actual behavior. Although compliance is always seen to be good, failure to follow policies and procedures and other attempts to circumvent controls may be an indication that the management controls mechanisms are cumbersome, insufficient, or inappropriate to the situation. Noncompliance may also be an indication that processes, policies, and procedures are out of date, especially if information systems have been implemented for ease of data management and controls. If use of policies and procedures and program management plans was not already reviewed as part of Module 4 – Compliance, it can be reviewed in this module. Interviews, documentation, and process mapping can be used to identify areas of noncompliance and their root causes.

A common challenge in the management of projects, especially ones that are moving very quickly or have a skeleton crew project team, is the inability of project staff to keep up with administrative processes. Piles of papers begin to congregate and cascade on desks and in drawers, information on documents is not entered into electronic systems in a timely fashion, signatures are not obtained . . . all because people are too busy to do so and are attending so many meetings that they can't get other work done, let alone satisfy governance objectives. This is a timeliness issue that may ultimately impact the ability to retrieve documents, accuracy of data in reports, payment of vendors, issuance of contracts and change orders, performance of work, receipt of resources, reduction of liability, and more. Delays in complying with management controls requirements may be an indication that project team members are overburdened or the controls mechanisms need to be streamlined.

A review of project controls may include estimating and scheduling methodologies, report accuracy, forecasting and trending, use of a standardized work breakdown structure (WBS) and chart of accounts, integration and validation of cost, schedule, and status data from contractors, and development of a schedule of values (SOV) that is consistent across contracts, invoices, reports, and change orders. Flow of information is important, especially among projects, program, and portfolio. As mentioned in Chapter 2: Discussion, the development of metrics and benchmark data can be fraught with errors. It is appropriate in this module to review the methodologies that support metrics and benchmarking, including the physical measurement of performance and processes for data gathering. Also important to project performance is how project controls staff use their time. If they spend most of their day compiling data to produce reports and wrestling with information systems, they are not playing a proactive role in controlling the project.

Controls in project and organizational management would include oversight, organizational structure, claims and dispute resolution mechanisms (including mediation and arbitration), quality control and quality assurance approaches, document control and records management, safety management, and inspection. In a project performance review, other governance mechanisms and controls that can be reviewed include formal processes for the use and release of contingency, use of allowances and treatment of funds remaining, issue management, scope management, authority to commit to contracts/purchase orders, change order/variations management, and signature authority.

This may also include information about ethics, team culture, behavior, peer pressure, flexibility, ability to innovate, and autonomy. Organizational maturity and sophistication are more than just process; they have been linked to cohesive culture, positive attitude, and consistent leadership. Through interviews and observation, the consultant can learn a lot about the team atmosphere, conduct at meetings, relationships, morale, organizational politics, power structure, conflict, and freedom to speak and act that can address or identify many of the listed problems associated with the flow of information. While the reviewer does not need to comment on individual personalities or personal problems, the issues around flow of information are an indicator of problems in the project operation. Any suspicion about the flow of information may be linked with one of the three Es, namely *Efficiency*.

The reviewer can also study the behavior of the interviewee, their level of enthusiasm for their work and the project, and their degree of openness; resistance to review may even inspire the reviewer to look more deeply at a process or department. In terms of management controls and project performance, the reviewer can look for formal decision-making processes, decision-making authority, shared governance (group decision making instead of individual), bureaucracy, consistent leadership, and documentation of assumptions and available data to show that decisions made were based on the best information available at the time.

As contracting, procurement, and project delivery also impact time, cost, and relationships, a review of controls in this area may include processes for bid and pricing review, invoice review and approvals, expediting, and insurance, guarantees, prompt payment, and bonding. It is important to look at the vetting of and selection process for vendors, fabricators, suppliers, contractors, and subcontractors for consistency, fairness, and impartiality. Legal risks related to contracting and procurement may be evaluated in Module 3 – Risk, and the choice of delivery and contract mechanism may already have been reviewed as part of Module 1 – Planning. The reviewer can also look at the longevity of vendors, fabricators, and suppliers on the project for clues about the management or mismanagement of such relationships and metrics developed to assess the quality of service provision.

Knowledge is, itself, an illusion; there is common knowledge shared among the team, data captured, and reports generated. Some behavior can be verified, and the rest is anecdotal. Small cost increases or schedule delays might not be reported, either dismissed as not important enough to reveal or not divulged in the hope that the project team can recover if given enough time (aside: such recovery is a rarity). Issues and variations are eventually reported when the changes become too great or too late to ignore and can no longer be reversed or obscured. There is select knowledge provided to stakeholders, and there may be knowledge silos in different areas of the project organization as well. The project may even look different when seen from different stakeholder and team member perspectives. As a result, knowledge flow can be difficult to review.

There is other knowledge that is never elicited or shared, which often forms the basis for people's actions. We assume that people have the project's best interests at heart, and management controls purport to ensure this. Contract terms may even require best-for-project decision making to dissuade opportunistic behavior. We presume rational behavior where it might not exist. The truth is, we might never know the full story of the project. However, the reviewer has the ability to identify and report on issues that the project team cannot due to internal politics or culture. The specialist consultant brings insight, and many of the review findings can be elicited from the project team itself through questionnaires and interviews. Often the project team knows what is wrong and how to fix it, but they lack the authority, funds, and/or self-confidence to do so. By asking probing questions, the reviewer can bring project challenges to the forefront in such a way that they will be reported and considered instead of suppressed. The reviewer can then enable the discussion and visibility of issues the project team is unable to have and also create the opportunity for project team members to take a step back and reflect on their organization, thinking about what can be done better. Organizations will often be more inclined to listen to an external party than to their own team. This is usually because the project team is driven to defend their own actions ahead of doing what is best for the project. Here, the reviewer can identify good ideas and recommendations that have perhaps been passed over by project administration due to unwillingness to listen to their own team. These are some of the questions a reviewer can ask to draw out hidden knowledge:

- Is there anything that will make your job easier?
- How would you fix this/what would you do if you had the necessary power and money?
- What are your biggest successes? What are your biggest challenges?
- What is going well? What isn't going well?
- Who else should we speak with? What other document should we review?

Accounting, enterprise resource planning (ERP), project management, legacy systems, and other software programs may require customized 'bridge' programming, duplicate manual entry, and other workarounds to pull information from multiple sources, 'talk' to other systems, and create an overall framework that works effectively. A performance review of project management and other management controls systems can map processes and validate information, identifying input data sources and the uses of data output from the system. Findings from such a review can then be used to develop recommendations for improvements to the systems, such as data input inefficiencies and delays, accuracy of source and system data, mapping problems, input errors, output errors, and processes that are at risk for user and programmed error. The relationship between project management and financial accounting often has gaps in information transfer or difficulties in integration of systems. During a performance review, financial accounting items that can be reviewed include reconciliation issues, processes for asset accounting, fiscal-year constraints in accounting systems that impact project cost accounting, timeliness, and mapping of financial system codes of accounts to project cost accounting codes.

Because project management is given the authority to implement the project, they are also expected to provide periodic status reports to stakeholders and funding sources. However, depending on their role, different stakeholders require different types of information at different times. As the project proceeds through its life cycle, decision makers need to receive information that is meaningful to them, in language they understand, in a simple format, appropriately actionable, and received in a timely manner. Expectations of project reporting for top-level oversight will be quite different compared to the expectations of those immersed in the project, and program-wide reporting will differ considerably from project reporting. One-size-fits-all reports, or dashboard reports, will be almost useless to those who need more granular data about projects, whereas high-level stakeholders don't necessarily need such levels of detail. Reports may contain too much or too little information; they may be data rich but information poor. Data may be (intentionally or unintentionally) misrepresented, missing or otherwise incomplete, unreconciled, out of date, or simply inaccurate; this can be audited by tracing project reports back to their sources of data.

Finding one single format that successfully communicates project status to multiple stakeholder groups can also be a challenge. Communication, dissemination of information, and reporting, both internal and external, should be reviewed during the performance review for appropriateness of content and transparency, consistent format, usefulness, timeliness, and accuracy. The reviewer can also review the level of effort required to generate reports, data sources, and how reports are actually used in practice compared to their intended use. If project team members keep separate records or develop their own spreadsheets to supplement existing reports, this may be an indication that the existing reports are inaccurate or not useful.

Additional controls to review and related issues may include (but are not limited to):

- Use of technology controls for expenditure approvals routing
- Automation of reporting
- Redundant or ineffective controls
- Failure to reconcile the project management system with the financial (or other) system
- Missing policies and procedures
- Lack of reporting
- Color-of-money issues (segregation and reporting of expenditures by funding source)
- Centralized management of vendors
- Outdated information in systems and on websites
- Timely approval of change orders

These are just a few examples of management controls areas to review and potential impact from findings. Because there is such breadth and depth of activity in management controls and governance mechanisms, the auditor needs to prioritize performance audit activities accordingly.

Module 7 – Post-project

Every project has deliverables, and most projects produce something that has a life cycle of its own after the project itself has been completed and closed out and the project organization dissolved. It may be an asset, a product, an event, or something else. This module addresses project closeout, activities that may occur immediately after closeout, and other matters related to the project deliverables. Much of what is reviewed during project closeout and post-project is related to *Effectiveness* and capturing information for success of operations and future projects.

During project closeout, the project performance will be measured against project acceptance criteria defined during the initiation and development stages of the project. There will likely be documentation requirements and deliverables, such as warranty information, maintenance and operations manuals, FF&E (furniture, fixtures, and equipment) lists, final project cost accounting, and signature acceptance. Contracts and purchase orders will be closed out. For assets such as buildings and equipment, capitalization and depreciation will occur, including funds accounting and cost segregation for tax purposes. Purchased and built assets will begin their own life cycle, often tracked through an asset management system. Asset data regarding maintenance schedules, useful life, and other relevant information may be integrated with facilities management systems.

As with project paperwork and administration, sometimes the organization is moving too quickly to enable proper closeout of projects. The asset is in use, product is being produced, and the project team may have splintered and moved on as each person or company satisfied their obligations on the project. There might be more pressing things to do at the time, or there might be nobody left to do the work, but formal closeout of projects is necessary to the organization from administrative, financial, and legal perspectives. Closeout of contracts prevents future claims against the Owner. Capture of project financial information enables fiscal year-end accounting and capitalization of assets. Some project managers (and legal departments) are experts at squirreling away funds. Release of contingency and remainders from allowances enables the released funds to be used on new projects. Most importantly, the filing of official paperwork with regulatory agencies can prevent the delay or cancellation of future projects, even many years down the line. For example, a building may require renovation, but failure to have filed project closeout paperwork from the original construction project 20 years ago may become an obstacle to the current renovation because the original project architect, inspector, and/or structural engineer have died and cannot provide required signatures. Government bureaucracy is simply not equipped to handle such problems. The consultant, in reviewing project closeout, can validate whether all required project closeout paperwork was filed in a timely manner.

After all contracts and purchase orders have been closed, project final data (such as total cost and performance metrics) can be collected to be used as historical data and benchmarks for future projects. Contractors, consultants, vendors, and suppliers may be evaluated for their performance on the project and those records kept for use by procurement on future bids and projects. When capturing project history, the project team needs to ensure that they avoid retrospective distortion of the facts and focus on hard data. For programs comprised of multiple projects, there may be an opportunity to identify patterns that occurred across all projects.

Lessons learned may be collected and will need to be recorded in as much detail as possible to enable search and retrieval for future projects; the mechanisms used for managing lessons learned vary from spreadsheets and physical binders with printed reports to more sophisticated databases. It is well known that lessons-learned mechanisms can be cumbersome and a challenge to maintain. The usability of this information is crucial, else the capture of lessons learned and historical data will be fruitless. Lessons-learned systems need to be carefully managed, assigned an owner, and periodically cleaned up lest they fall into disrepair and disuse – this, in itself, is a lesson learned.

Once the project is delivered and the deliverables are being used, the Owner may wish to conduct a final survey of user satisfaction. This may help identify usability issues, repair and maintenance needs (and warranty invocation), future adaptations and modifications, and additional lessons learned for future projects. A post-project review may be required for benefits evaluation or specialty certifications such as building environmental ratings and sustainability.

Post-project elements to consider reviewing for this module may include:

- Defect, repair, and warranty issues
- Commissioning and testing issues
- Missing equipment manuals
- Failure to conduct staff training related to new equipment and systems
- Adequacy of facilities management system related to new equipment and software
- Accuracy of asset management system related to purchased and built assets
- Close out documentation and as-built drawings
- Functionality of methods used to capture, track, search, and retrieve lessons learned

- Usability, completeness, normalization, subjectivity, and granularity of historic data
- Owner satisfaction with the project handover process

These are just a few examples of project, deliverables, and management issues that may surface toward the end of the project life cycle. The reviewers need to take care, regarding project closeout and post-project matters, to ensure that performance review elements are specifically related to project performance. Some of the elements listed (facilities and asset management systems specifically) may be reviewed relative to project assets but would require a separate review for an even deeper and broader review of their functionality and performance organization-wide.

Module 8 – Special issues

The authors note that not every issue fits neatly into a box, so we have created a module specifically for such review elements that might not have been addressed in the other modules. These could be any concerns unique to the project or organizational concerns related to the project that require special consideration and have the potential to affect project *Economy, Efficiency,* or *Effectiveness.*

If expenditure audit is required by law or funding source, it can be included in this module to distinguish it from the compliance module. However, this module is not designed to accommodate review elements that should be scoped as a separate engagement; these are discussed in the next section as performance review exclusions.

Where previous reviews have been conducted, the status of the resolution of previous findings can be addressed here; too often, reports and findings are shelved, resolution of findings is not performed because the project team is too busy fighting fires elsewhere, or the project lacks the time and monetary resources to make it happen. Failure to resolve findings has an impact on project performance by effectively preventing continuous improvement. Such failure may be a waste of the monies and time spent on the review. Where findings are not resolved due to lack of funds, reduction in priority or ROI, or other reasons, the reviewer should obtain justification and evidence of approvals for such decisions made. A formal decision to not act on findings is itself resolution of a finding.

The reviewers could, here, also comment on their experiences in conducting the review if the reviewer experienced issues that obstructed performance of the review. Examples of such issues include documents not provided, interviewees unavailable, and/or access to the project or organization otherwise restricted.

Project performance review exclusions

While it can be tempting to include as much as possible in the review scope, doing so can be detrimental to the performance review process and results. For example, when soliciting proposals from consulting firms, certain firms may be better at some review elements than others, and it might not be possible to get one firm (or team of firms) to do everything. Some types of review may be specific to project timing or may be related to legal issues. Where review and analysis elements can be segregated as a specialized engagement, especially if they require technical expertise, they should be procured separately.

When developing the performance audit scope, the Owner should at all times keep in mind the intent of the performance audit and exclude any audit elements that do not serve that purpose. The Owner also needs to understand the specific skill sets required to conduct certain types of audit and segregate those as appropriate. Timing, available data, legal implications, and other issues may also apply when determining what to include in or exclude from the performance audit scope.

This section of the book explores a number of specific types of reviews that commonly occur on projects. It is not uncommon for a specific type of review to be required for a particular reason, which might not be included as part of the performance review. For instance, financial audits and environmental health and safety audits may be required by financiers or even required under state or federal law.

In cases where there occurs an overlap with other audits and/or reviews, it may be prudent for the reviewer to acknowledge those past or future reviews and reports. The reviewer should examine the extent to which other reviews guided the scope of the performance review and whether the performance review filled a gap or otherwise supplemented previous reviews. The performance reviewer should, at a minimum, reflect on the extent to which they relied on the findings of other reviews and/or audits and list those reports in an appendix in their own performance review report. Findings from the performance review may concur with or differ from findings from other reviews and/or audits. In such instances, the findings will likely be due to the supporting documentation received and should be noted. Such findings may also reflect organizational changes that occurred since the review or audit, such as the resolution of the findings from previous reviews or audits, and should be commended.

In the paragraphs that follow, a description of a number of different types of audits is provided to guide the reviewer when scoping the performance review.

A *financial audit* evaluates financial reports and reporting processes, usually on an annual basis. A project may require reporting of the use of funds from various sources, and thus financial audit may be a requirement for project funding. Because financial audits are performed almost exclusively by accounting firms, this type of audit lends itself to being an engagement separate from the performance review. The authors note that many clients choose to conduct the project financial audit and project performance review concurrently but procured separately in order to attract consultants with appropriate expertise and skill sets. If financial audit is part of the scope of the performance review, financial audit standards will apply.

Fraud is any intentional act (or omission) designed to deceive others, resulting in the victim suffering a loss and/or the perpetrator (whether that be an individual or an entity) achieving some benefit or unfair or unlawful gain. Deception is a key element of fraud; examples include misappropriation of assets, fraudulent reporting, false charges (of time or money), and more. Auditors use software programs to detect fraud through duplication, irregularities, and pattern recognition. Unfortunately, compliance audits more frequently surface human error than fraud. The majority of fraudulent activity is identified through anonymous tips (often through a hotline or Inspector General office) or is accidentally discovered; accidental discovery is the primary means of fraud detection. Performance review is not necessarily a primary detection mechanism for fraud, although it is sometimes discovered during a review of controls compliance and/or efforts to circumvent controls. While performance reviewers may find evidence of fraud, internal controls and internal/external financial and controls audits are the predominant formal fraud-prevention and detection mechanisms. For this reason, an audit targeted specifically for fraud should be conducted as a separate engagement from the performance review.

Several types of review are similar to performance review, and address the three Es but are likely to be procured separately. Three of these are *value-for-money audits, stage gate reviews,* and *project health checks.*

Value-for-money (VfM) reviews are a well-known proxy for performance reviews, with a sharper focus specifically on the three Es, inputs, and outputs. As with performance reviews, there is no global standard for VfM reviews. Because it can be difficult to measure the three Es in the complex reality of projects, the VfM approach tends to gravitate toward the use of quantitative metrics, experiencing the same issues as previously discussed. Financial assessment and life cycle costing may be included in the VfM review scope and also nonfinancial aspects such as innovation, flexibility of operation, user benefits, incentives, monitoring, and even softer elements such as contribution to the greater social good. VfM reviews experience many of the same challenges as performance reviews, especially the use of best practices checklists. Again, performance reviews can be used to supplement VfM reviews and are not intended to replace them.

Stage gate reviews, also called *gateway* or *phase gate reviews,* are an iterative evaluation methodology that occurs at specific phases of a project, often a pass/fail mechanism that requires a passing grade for the project to progress to the next phase. As mentioned earlier, performance review can be used to supplement stage gate reviews and is not intended to replace the stage gate project approach. Stage gate reviews focus keenly on strategic priorities, controls, and objectives realization. The typical stage gate framework includes considerable analysis at the front end of a project, including project definition, business case analysis, and project development/design, more deeply than would be conducted in a performance review.

Project health checks are the least defined and structured of the three and were developed specifically to evaluate projects in a universe of evaluation methodologies that continues to be less project specific and more organization specific. The intent of the project health check is to look deeper than the traditional time–cost–quality triangle. As with VfM and stage gate reviews, there exists no standardized process for project health checks. Variability of approach is even greater than with VfM and stage gate reviews because, whereas the majority of VfM and stage gate review methodologies have been developed and implemented by government agencies, project health checks have typically been marketed and conducted by consulting firms. It is considerably less formal than other types of project review and may have a much less rigorous and documentable approach. Many approaches to project health checks rely on the use of metrics. Project health checks tend to focus heavily on project management procedures and less on financial analysis and are well known for their dependence on best practices checklists.

Value engineering and *constructability reviews* are typically conducted during the project design and engineering and are related to both optimization of design and peer review. A value engineering workshop will typically follow a systematic methodology for questioning the function of design elements and their associated cost. It is a very useful exercise in addressing the *Economy* part of project performance and may also touch on analysis of *Efficiency* (especially for machinery and equipment) and *Effectiveness* of performance. Constructability review offers a detailed analysis of construction plans and specifications, seeking opportunities for uncovering design problems that would impact construction, and improving bid documents, thus reducing change orders and disputes. Both of these types of reviews must be conducted by specialists and engineers, and as such they are not a good fit with performance review.

An in-depth formal *enterprise architecture* (EA) process would not likely be included in a project performance review. EA is a methodology already familiar to heavy manufacturing, government, and aerospace programs. The EA approach involves writing a detailed and rigorous description of the structure of an enterprise, breaking down the enterprise into modules and then reassembling them (conceptually) in context. In this sense, the structured EA approach is very similar to value engineering. The process also involves documenting financial, social, and technical aspects of the system and the relationships between them. This information is then used to identify system risks and opportunities, and enhance maturity. The focus, in the project context, is on optimization and locating and resolving root causes for performance issues.

A *risk identification workshop* and formal modeling process, as described in Module 3 – Risk, would also likely be procured separately from a performance review. This is due to the specialized skill set needed for workshop facilitation and risk elicitation and the targeted nature of the exercise. Risk analysis has specific timing needs and requires project team member and end user participation. Output from the risk workshop and analysis may be used to inform the performance review. Any opportunity risks that have been identified may have treatment plans involving engineering and constructability type of reviews.

Environmental, health, and safety (EHS) audits and reporting may be required by law. The audit assesses the environmental impact of work processes, makes the workplace safer by identifying dangerous situations and practices, and addresses other regulatory compliance. EHS inspectors must be certified and follow very specific procedures. Due to these requirements, it makes sense to perform EHS audits separately. These audits are in addition to the daily or weekly EH&S inspections typically carried out by the project team.

A *quality assurance and quality control (QA/QC) review* is tasked with identifying deviations from specifications and/or standards with the intent to ensure project deliverables meet project objectives and requirements. There should be a project-specific QA/QC plan; quality assurance (QA) is process oriented and focuses on the way things are done, whereas quality control (QC) is product oriented and confirms that the results of the project are as expected or promised. Quality issues may be found during any phase of the project life cycle, even during project initiation and development. Project work may be reviewed in progress, resulting in the opportunity to make improvements, or may be reviewed upon submittal for acceptance. Although there may be similarities between QA/QC and performance review, QA/QC review often requires specialized skill sets that make it appropriate to procure separately. Output from both quality assurance and quality control may be used to inform the performance review.

If something has gone wrong on the project and it becomes a matter of legal concern, there may be a need for a *forensic review or audit*. Although a forensic review does, technically, review the performance of an element, the project, or the resulting asset, it is usually conducted with the intent to investigate, diagnose, and understand what has happened as part of some claim or potential litigation. Specifically due to the legal applications of this type of review and the necessary scientific rigor required in the likelihood that information will be used as evidence in a court of law or as part of expert testimony, a forensic review should be conducted separately from a performance audit. Note: Findings from the performance review may be used to inform a forensic review.

Similar to forensic review, but without the legal focus, *technical audit* also seeks to investigate, diagnose, understand, and remedy a project problem or defect. It may be a peer review by someone within the company or by a third-party consultant. Often, that problem is related to design, engineering, software, machinery, or equipment. The review may include elements of QA/QC, cost, and schedule. Again, this type of review must be conducted by specialists and engineers, and as such the scope of the technical audit is not a good fit with performance review.

Sustainability audit is a fairly new concept and depends heavily on the organization's definitions of sustainability. In project terms, sustainability may be related to energy consumption, technical and financial support, environmental impact, and more. In the specific instance of capital projects, some building certification programs (such as LEED – Leadership in Energy and Environmental Design, United States Green Building Council – and BREEAM – Building Research Establishment Environmental Assessment Methodology) or the Australian Green Star rating require an audit to verify the design and performance of elements applicable to sustainable sites, water *Efficiency*, energy and atmosphere, materials and resources use, and indoor environmental quality. Because the definitions and scopes of sustainability audit are variable, require specialized knowledge, and may be specific to certification requirements, sustainability audits are best conducted separately from performance review. Parts of the performance review may be useful inputs to the sustainability audit.

The reviews and audits listed are just some of the examples of scopes of work that would likely be procured and conducted separately from the performance review. In the experience of the authors, other project reviews are an important resource to consider when planning and undertaking performance reviews. It would be wise for both the client and the reviewer to reflect on the overlaps and gaps that exist between other past and future reviews and use this information to improve the scope of the performance review.

5 Summary

The future of project performance review

Performance review is still an emerging profession that has not yet become firmly institutionalized. It may never fully mature, because approaches to audit and review through the decades can be seen to evolve in parallel with strategic management theory, albeit with a slight time lag.[1] However, advancements in technology will undoubtedly make an impact.

Improvements in project management systems will increase the use of automated controls in procurement, expenditures, and change management, including routing documents for approvals. The technology currently exists but is not widely utilized; in the authors' experience, most project oversight still prefers a paper trail to an electronic trail. Such automated controls will simplify the compliance element of project review, and auditors will have the ability to generate an exception report at the press of a button. Use of such systems will depend on the level of sophistication, budget, and size of the project organization and owner entity.

An increase in the global availability of data will cause a trend toward benchmarking and business metrics, with the associated risks of doing so as discussed earlier in Chapter 2. Validation of project history and proof of impact to project performance may include the review of externally available data from reliable sources, such as extreme weather, currency fluctuations, news reports, and political activity. We are entering an era wherein the reviewer might no longer be reliant solely on client data.

Advancements in data capture and increased use of information systems in accounting and project management will naturally impact the audit profession and show considerable promise for performance review. On-demand real-time accessibility to data will likely reduce the time lag between data input and availability of data for analysis, which will resolve some of the challenges experienced by auditors due to timing. As for the quality and availability of data from the entirety of ERM and project management systems, the performance review of the future may well be able to test the entire population of project data instead of relying on sampling. By testing the entire population of data (such as expenditures), the reviewer may be able to offer guaranteed assurance instead of just reasonable assurance. This data will then lend itself to analysis and modeling, predictive analytics, pattern identification, and attempts at forecasting, some of which will blur the lines among auditing, evaluation, and consulting. However, the same challenges will exist regarding forecasting as discussed in Chapter 2 of this book. The sheer volume of available data will enable continuous monitoring and review of both the organization and project and a time-lapse picture of performance. The authors note this scenario predicts an extreme focus on quantitative measures and caution that qualitative elements of review should not be sacrificed.

As the practices of performance review and audit continue to evolve and become more sophisticated, questions arise about whether a distinction should be made between a review of project implementation and a review of achievement of project objectives. It can be argued that the two efforts require drastically different skill sets and approaches, one as an exercise in compliance and the other more focused on evaluation. Currently, those two concepts are intertwined in performance reviews, along with the concepts of compliance and accountability. The future of performance review may see the two approaches take different directions, or they may continue to merge.

These are just some of the many possibilities for the performance review of the future. Who knows what else awaits?

Closing comments

This book is intended to serve several purposes. It offers a flexible model for both performance review and audit and some guidance regarding how and why to review different project elements. It also provides advice on how to scope and procure a performance review. Ultimately, all of these are efforts to close the audit expectation gap regarding stakeholder understanding of the purpose, breadth, and depth of performance reviews. We advocate a carefully considered approach to scoping and conducting performance reviews, which will yield opportunities, reduced risks, and findings that offer significant ROI to both the project reviewed and the Owner organization.

The authors hope the Nalewaik-Mills Performance Review Method contribution to the body of knowledge for performance review will result in greater maturity in performance review methods and better public awareness of the significant value of conducting performance reviews and audits. Ultimately, deeper understanding and greater acceptance of performance reviews and audits as project management best practice may lead to new, appropriate, and sensible developments in performance audit standards and regulatory requirements. It is also hoped that improved recognition of the profession will yield a culture of learning supported by formal education at the university level, professional development seminars and training, dedicated journals, research, professional institutions, and certification programs.

Note

1 Nalewaik, A. (2015). Linking Cost Engineering with Strategy and Project Performance. *Centre for Excellence in Project Management (CEPM) 22nd Global Symposium 2015*, November.

Further reading

Published works and presentations by the authors

- Nalewaik, A. (2012). Systemic Audit and Substantive Evaluation in the Built Environment. *AACE International's Source Magazine*, 4(August 2012), 26–33.
- Nalewaik, A. (2013). Factors Affecting Capital Program Performance Audit Findings. *International Journal of Managing Projects in Business*, 6(3), 615–623.
- Nalewaik, A. (2015). Linking Cost Engineering with Strategy and Project Performance. *Centre for Excellence in Project Management (CEPM) 22nd Global Symposium 2015*, November.
- Nalewaik, A. and Mills, A. (2014). The Path to Assurance: An Analysis of Project Performance Methodologies. *Procedia – Social and Behavioral Sciences*, 119(2014), 105–114.
- Nalewaik, A. and Mills, A. (2015). Project Performance Audit: Enhanced Protocols for Triple Bottom Line Results. *Procedia – Social and Behavioral Sciences*, 194(2015), 134–145.
- Nalewaik-Mills Performance Review Method, copyright by the authors, 2014.

Other recommended reading

- Adams, M. B. (1994). Agency Theory and the Internal Audit. *Managerial Auditing Journal*, 9(8), 8–12.
- Blalock, A. B. (1999) Vol 5(2): 117–149. Evaluation Research and the Performance Management Movement: From Estrangement to Useful Integration? *Evaluation*, 5(17).
- CEAD AMS Unit. (2015). *"Performance Audit Manual"*, Luxembourg: European Court of Auditors.
- Committee of Sponsoring Organizations of the Treadway Commission (COSO). www.coso.org/guidance.htm
- Comptroller General of the United States. (2007). *Government Auditing Standards*. United States Government Accountability Office, July 2011 Revision, GAO-07–731G.
- Deis, D. R. and Giroux, G. A. (1992). Determinants of Audit Quality in the Public Sector. *The Accounting Review*, 67(3), 462–479.

- English, Linda (2007). Performance Audit of Australian Public Private Partnerships: Legitimising Government Policies or Providing Independent Oversight? *Financial Accountability and Management*, 23(3), 313–336.
- Francis, J. R. (2011). A Framework for Understanding and Researching Audit Quality. *Auditing*, 30(2), 125–152.
- Holmquist, J. and Barklund-Larsson, U. (1996). New Public Management, Performance Auditing, and How Auditors Can Contribute to Performance Improvement. In *Performance Auditing and the Modernisation of Government*. Paris: Organisation for Economic Co-operation and Development (OECD).
- Hubbard, Douglas W. (2009). *The Failure of Risk Management: Why It's Broken and How To Fix It*. Hoboken, NJ: John Wiley and Sons Inc.
- International Organisation of Supreme Audit Institutions (INTOSAI) Professional Standards Committee. (2015, September). *International Standards of Supreme Audit Institutions (ISSAI) 3000: Performance Audit Standard (Exposure Draft)*. Copenhagen: INTOSAI.
- International Standards Office. (2011). *ISO 19011 – Guidelines for Auditing Management Systems*. Geneva: ISO Copyright Office.
- Low, K.-Y. (2004). The Effects of Industry Specialization on Audit Risk Assessments and Audit-Planning Decisions. *The Accounting Review*, 79(1), 201–219.
- March, James G. and Sutton, Robert I. (1997). Organizational Performance as a Dependent Variable. *Organization Science*, 8(6), 698–706.
- Newcomer, K. E. (1994). Opportunities and Incentives for Improving Program Quality: Auditing and Evaluating. *Public Administration Review*, 54(2), 147–154.
- Oakes, Graham (2008). *Project Reviews, Assurance, and Governance*. Aldershot: Gower Publishing Limited.
- Sloan, N. (1996). The Objectives and Performance Measurement of Performance Audit. *Performance Auditing and the Modernisation of Government*. Paris: Organisation for Economic Co-operation and Development.
- Taleb, Nassim Nicholas (2007). *The Black Swan: The Impact of the Highly Improbable*. New York: Random House.
- Technical Board. (2006). *Total Cost Management Framework*. Morgantown, WV: AACE International.
- Williams III, Frank P., McShane, Marilyn D. and Sechrest, Dale (1994). Barriers to Effective Performance Review: The Seduction of Raw Data. *Public Administration Review*, 54(6), 537–542.

Index

Acceptance 49, 73, 80
Accountability 2–3, 7–10, 40, 62–63, 67, 83
Accountant (CPA) 4, 32, 34
Accounting 4, 7–8, 16, 32, 71, 73, 82
Accuracy 1, 7–8, 14, 26, 54, 63, 68–69, 71, 72, 74
Agency theory 27–28
Agreed-upon procedures 9, 29, 33–34
Allowances 69, 73
Approvals 8, 14, 46, 49, 63
Asset 45, 64, 71, 73–75
Assessment 10–11
Assurance 1–4, 10, 36, 83
Attestation 12
Audit 1, 4, 7, 9–11, 62, 67, 82–83
Audit criteria 62
Audit expectations gap 5, 51, 54
Audit findings 5, 12–13, 18, 26–27, 29, 31, 38, 40, 70, 76–77
Audit history 7–8
Audit objectives 34
Audit standards 1, 5, 7, 10–13, 34, 39, 62
Authority 2, 69–71

Baseline 38, 48
Benchmarking 4, 20–22, 26, 33, 39, 41, 46, 69, 74, 82
Best for project 71
Best practices 3–5, 22–24, 39, 68, 78
Bias 17–18, 20
Bid 70, 74, 79
Budget 25–26, 40, 48–49, 63, 82

Bureaucracy 16, 67, 70, 73
Business case 48, 78

Cash flow 50, 66
Causation 21, 23
Certification 4, 81
Change management 2, 40, 45, 49, 63–64, 82
Change orders 68–69, 79
Checklists 5, 8–9, 22–24, 30, 36, 43, 62, 78
Claims and disputes 34, 69, 73, 79–80
Closeout 38, 43, 46, 73–75
Commissioning 38, 74
Communication 52–54, 62, 67, 72
Compliance 1, 4, 8, 9, 10–11, 13, 34, 41, 44–45, 49, 62–63, 76, 78, 83
Compliance audit 1, 4–5, 8, 12, 30, 34, 62, 78
Confidence 1, 14, 70
Constraint 46, 65
Constructability review 79–80
Construction audit 4
Consultants/consulting 3, 5–6, 12, 14, 17, 22–33, 37–39, 83
Context 14
Contingency 57, 69, 73
Continuous improvement 6, 10, 21, 36, 76
Contract 4, 8, 45, 48, 50, 59, 63, 67–70, 73–74
Controls 2–3, 7, 9–10, 23, 40, 44–45, 49, 54, 56, 66–72, 78, 82
Correlation 21, 23
Cost 49, 65, 67, 69–70, 72, 79, 81

Critical questioning 9, 39
Critical path 50
Critical success factors 9, 20
Culture 67, 69–70

Data 18, 21–22, 24, 26, 65, 68–72, 74, 82–83
Deception 8, 20, 77
Decision-making 2, 6, 20, 24–25, 46, 48–49, 54, 63–64, 67, 70
Defect 80
Delay 65, 68, 70, 73
Deliverable 73–74, 80
Delivery 48, 50, 70
Deming cycle 39–40, 43, 52, 56
Design 48, 78–81
Development 44, 48, 78
Documentation 8, 12–13, 15, 18–19, 22, 24, 37, 40, 49–50, 57, 59, 63, 66–68, 70, 73–74, 76–77, 82
Document control 69
Document request 15, 18–19
Drawings 74
Due diligence 61
Duration 15, 30–31

Early warning system 56, 59
Earned value 25–26
Economic analysis 48
Economy 1, 3, 9, 11, 14, 21, 24, 29, 36, 39, 41–42, 48, 53, 59, 63, 65, 67, 76, 79
Education 4–5
Effectiveness 1, 3, 9, 11, 14, 21, 23–24, 29, 36, 39, 41–42, 48, 51, 54, 59, 65, 67, 73, 76, 79
Efficiency 1, 3, 9, 11, 14, 21, 24, 29, 36, 39, 41–42, 48, 53, 59, 64–65, 69, 76, 79, 81
Efficiency audit 8
Engagement 11–12, 27–29
Engineering 48, 79–81
Enterprise architecture 79
Enterprise risk management 39, 82
Environmental health and safety 80
Errors 8, 14, 27–28, 32, 40, 63–64, 69, 71, 78
Estimate 25, 48, 69
Ethics 3, 12, 17, 28, 69
Evaluation 5, 7–11, 32, 65, 78, 83
Evidence 80

Exceptions 64, 82
Exclusion 76
Execution 44–46, 48
Expenditure 2, 4, 8, 13–15, 27, 29, 30–31, 36, 40–41, 59, 62–64, 72, 76, 82
Expenditure audit 1, 4, 8, 11, 76
Experience 2, 5, 11, 25, 27–28, 30, 32–34
Expert 2, 25, 28, 33, 57, 80
Expert opinion 25, 57

Failure 3–4, 9, 46, 51, 56
Financial audit 1, 5, 7, 9, 12, 32, 34, 77
Findings 18, 26–27, 29, 31, 38, 40, 70, 76–77
Fiscal year 16, 30–31, 38, 71, 73
Flexibility 3, 5, 36, 38, 78
Forecasting 20, 24–26, 43, 69, 83
Forensic audit 33, 40, 49, 80
Fraud 8, 12–13, 30, 59, 77–78
Frugality 9
Funding 2, 44, 46, 48, 50, 62, 64, 69, 72–73, 76–77
Future 1, 6, 9–10, 11, 15, 24–26, 43, 48, 51, 63, 73–74, 77, 81–83

Goals 1, 5–6, 9–10, 20, 42, 46, 48, 67
Governance 13, 16, 23, 36, 38, 40, 42, 44, 56, 62, 64, 67–68, 70, 72

History 3, 14, 18, 24, 38, 53, 66, 74–75, 82

Independence 12–13, 17
Information technology systems 66, 68–69, 71, 82
Initiation 43–44, 48
Innovation 8, 16, 69, 78
Input and output 10, 78
Inspector general 59, 78
Insurance 56, 59, 70
Integrity 8, 13, 28
Intent 1, 14, 20, 22, 27, 34–35, 63–64, 72, 77, 80
Internal audit 4, 7, 9, 18
Internal controls 8, 45, 64–65, 78
Invoices 14, 63, 69–70
Issue management 69

Judgment 2–3, 14–15, 26, 57

Key performance indicators 4, 9, 20
Knowledge 23, 32–33, 66, 70–71

Leadership 16, 54, 69–70
Learning 10
Lessons learned 33, 38, 41, 43, 66, 74
Liability 68
Lifecycle 6, 9, 16, 31, 36, 38, 40, 43, 48, 67, 73, 75, 78, 80
Litigation 12, 80

Materiality 17, 26–27, 32, 38, 41, 64, 68
Metrics 4, 9, 20–21, 26, 29, 38, 69–70, 74, 78–79, 82
Milestone 2, 5, 21, 23, 40, 43, 50, 67
Monitoring 4, 9, 20, 26, 28, 54, 59, 78, 83
Monte Carlo model 57

Objectives 2, 46, 57, 78, 80, 83
Open book 18
Operational audit 1, 9, 39
Opportunistic behavior 70
Opportunity 56–57, 59, 61, 65, 68, 71, 79–80
Optimism 17–18, 25
Optimization 6, 10, 42, 79
Organization 6, 71, 73, 79
Organization chart 69
Organizational maturity 1, 6, 10, 26, 31, 41, 43, 79, 83
Overconfidence 17, 57
Oversight 1, 2, 6, 9, 16, 54, 69, 82

Performance 20–21, 24, 48, 52, 62, 68, 73–75, 79
Performance measurement 4, 9, 20, 39, 46
Planning 24, 44, 46, 48–49, 57, 66
Policies and procedures 2, 4, 8, 10, 16, 41–42, 45, 49, 62–64, 67–68, 72
Portfolio 11, 16, 69
Post-project 73–75
Predictability 6
Pricing 70
Priorities 67, 72, 78
Processes 2, 31, 38–40, 45, 48, 54, 63–64, 67–71
Procurement 26, 41, 48, 67, 70, 74, 82
Professional organizations 3
Program 11, 15–16, 69, 74

Progress 20, 24, 26, 29, 38, 54, 78, 80
Project 2, 11
Project controls 8, 45, 63, 67
Project health check 78–79
Project management 3–4, 16, 23–24, 38–39, 45, 56, 63, 67, 71, 82
Project management office 15–16
Purchase order 45, 73–74

Quality 9–11, 13, 24, 48, 67, 79, 82
Quality assurance/quality control 5, 10, 13, 69, 80–81

Reasonability 3, 9, 41, 63, 68, 83
Reconciliation 71
Recovery 63–64, 70
Regulatory requirements 4, 8–9, 31, 36, 44, 46, 51, 54, 59, 62, 64, 73, 80, 84
Report – Review 31
Reporting – Project 22, 24–25, 38, 67, 69–72
Requirements 41–42, 44–46, 48, 50, 52, 62, 68, 80
Relationships 79
Resolution 13, 31, 41, 54, 76–77
Resources 1, 10, 38–39, 41–42, 44–46, 48, 64–66, 76, 81
Return on investment 11, 49, 76
Rigor 80
Risk 2, 5–6, 10, 20, 25–26, 30, 36, 38–39, 44–45, 48, 56–61, 63, 65–66, 79–80, 82
Risk tolerance 36, 53–54, 57, 59
Root cause 68, 79
Routing 82
Rules 2, 8

Safety 69
Sampling 13–15, 83
Schedule 48, 65, 69–70, 81
Schedule of values 69
Scope – project 48–50, 69
Scope – review 16, 26, 28–29, 33–37, 39–43, 62, 76–77, 81
Segregation 8, 73
Self-assessment 17
Single audit 33–34
Skills/skillset 2, 5, 7–8, 77, 83
Social sciences 9
Software 68, 71, 74, 78, 81
Solicitation 26, 32–34, 76

Sophistication 82
Specialization 33, 76, 80–81
Specifications 48, 79–80
Staff 66, 68–69
Stage gate review 39, 78–79
Stakeholder 1, 3, 5, 10, 18, 29–30, 36, 38, 42, 44–46, 48–49, 51–55, 61, 64, 70–72
Stewardship 3, 39
Strategic management 7, 9, 82
Strategic objectives 6, 44, 48
Strategy 8, 9, 20, 24, 38, 44, 46, 49, 82
Subjectivity 51, 57, 75
Success 3–4, 9, 20, 24, 36, 42, 46, 48, 51, 62, 65, 71
Sustainability 74, 81
Systems audit 1, 8
Systems 2, 30, 67, 71, 73–75, 82–83

Technical audit 80, 81
Testing 13–15, 26, 74, 83

Time 70, 79
Timeline 68, 72, 74
Timing 30, 40, 76, 82
Total Cost Management 39
Total quality management 39
Training 3, 66, 74
Transparency 2–3, 63, 67, 72
Trend 14, 25–26, 38, 57, 69, 82

Validation 8–9, 11, 18, 69, 82
Value engineering 39, 42, 48, 79
Value for money 3, 78–79
Variability 6, 16, 79
Variance analysis 26

Warranty 74
Waste 8–9, 42, 65, 76
Work breakdown structure 69
Workpapers 12

Yellow book audit 33–34

Printed in the United States
by Baker & Taylor Publisher Services